D1602394

Lost at CEO

Praise for Carl Cox, Lost at CEO

"Success in business is predictable if you know what determines it…thought-provoking insights on how to turn around a failing business, or, to take an ordinary business to extraordinary. If you are a CEO or business owner, and you only have time to read one book this year, it should be Lost at CEO."

Jim Britt, 15X Best-selling Author, Keynote Speaker

"A no BS, practical, and honest look at the confusion, frustrations, and glory of the life and responsibility of a CEO. This book will make you laugh, cry and most importantly, will inspire and empower you to make pivotal shifts that make life better for everyone involved."

Isabelle Mercier, Co-Founder & CEO of LeapZone Strategies, TEDx Speaker

"I have decades of experience working with teams trying to use the overwhelming number of frameworks and tools out there. Every CEO will instantly relate to the characters in this uniquely approachable yet illuminating story. Carl provides the clearest approach yet to navigating the business complexity that sends many companies off course."

Kevin Ilcisin, Ph.D. SVP Strategy and Corporate Development, NI

"Packed with business and leadership wisdom that is useful to most of us who lead people and companies, and then wrapped in a compelling story that keeps us reading."

Antoni Lacinai, Global Speaker, Author and Entrepreneur

"The storytelling and the actual explanation of the process is simply amazing. It brought me tears, laughter, and a deep sense of pride...I read it straight through."

Scott Ballard, Trusted Advisor, Confidence Coach, Former CEO

"If you desire to become a strategic leader, then Carl Cox is your mentor. Carl clearly understands the intricacies of strategic leadership and 'unfurls' these principles in this book."

Dr. William E. Morgan, President at Parker University

"A compelling story showcasing powerful examples of how to never give up on finding a better solution to lead your team and companies to success."

Terry Sidford, Author, TEDx Speaker, and Professional Coach, Create Your Life International

"An engrossing story with wisdom not only for a CEO but also lower level managers."

Dr. Bill Conerly, Senior Contributor to Forbes, Economist, Author, and Business Consultant

"Carl has a superpower of laying out how to achieve lofty goals in a simple and easy to use format...he connects the dots between the entrepreneurial challenges of reality, metrics, emotion, and execution to help us finally do strategy the right way."

Dr. Jeremy Weisz, CEO of Rise25 and Founder of Inspired Insider Podcast

"This book brings every CEO back to port when they feel they are lost at sea."

Mark Lewis, Executive Coach & President of Communique,
#1 Best Selling Author, Give a Damn

"Lost at CEO paints a precise picture of a leader seeking answers for how to make an annual strategic planning effort really work - this time...make a place for this work on your bookshelf ...adopt its vocabulary - before your next strategic planning session".

Jerry Vieira, Certified Management Consultant,
Author, The Consultancy Navigator

Lost at CEO

An Entrepreneur's Guide to Strategy

Carl J. Cox

Published by Game Changer Publishing

Paperback ISBN: 979-8-9880752-9-5
Hardcover ISBN: 978-1-961189-24-9
Digital ISBN: 978-1-961189-25-6

www.GameChangerPublishing.com

DEDICATION

This book is dedicated to my wonderful wife, Sarah, and our four amazing children, Ashley, Zachary, Tyler, and Abigail, who have supported me through my own entrepreneurial journey.

Read This First

Just to say thanks for buying and reading my book, I would like to give you a few free bonus gifts, no strings attached!

Scan for Book Gifts

Lost at CEO

An Entrepreneur's Guide to Strategy

Carl J. Cox

www.GameChangerPublishing.com

Foreword

Much like you, I suspect, I'm a reader. Each year, I set the goal to read 100 books. I've hit that goal—and exceeded it—for over twenty years. I read it all—poetry, fiction, economics, politics, history, biography, novels, education—any topic that I think will make me a better thinker, better father, better husband, better manager, better person. I'm here for that journey.

As a devoted reader of business literature, and a published author in the field myself, I am constantly in search of insightful stories that can inspire personal and professional growth. *Lost at CEO* certainly did not disappoint in that regard. This leadership fable speaks directly to business executives who have reached the common crossroads of "What do I do next?"

When Carl first approached me to write the foreword for this book, I was deeply honored. Our work as consultants to CEOs and authors of business books complements each other perfectly. As we share the same goal of helping CEOs become the best leaders they can be, I was excited to add my voice to the story that Carl has crafted here.

As consultants and authors, we are constantly helping company leaders focus on achieving their goals despite endless distractions, problems, and crises. However, even after finding focus, CEOs often lack a roadmap for maintaining it. This is where *Lost at CEO* comes in. It is a practical guide for clarifying your focus, designing a strategy that is actionable, delegating work to your team, and most importantly, moving the needle as a leader. I see it as the perfect complement to my book, *A CEO Only Does Three Things: Finding Your Focus in the C-Suite.*

Regardless of what stage of entrepreneurship or company growth you are in, this book provides valuable insights. From solopreneurs to CEOs of $50 million companies, *Lost at CEO* offers actionable takeaways for everyone. As someone who has been a CEO for many years, and has worked with countless others, I found myself nodding along with the pages and learning something new with each turn.

This book is filled with real-world scenarios that are incredibly relatable, making it an essential guide for modern-day CEOs who face multiple pressures. Although the principles outlined in the book are versatile enough to apply to any business, the storytelling is specific enough to help you feel seen and understood.

In Jack's story, I found many strategies that I hope to implement in my own business. Most importantly, I saw myself represented in this story. The sleepless nights, the sacrifices, the impossible decisions, and the feeling of being stuck were all familiar to me. This book provides a roadmap to help you navigate these challenges and make strategic planning more straightforward without adding more to your plate ... and most importantly, shows you that while you may feel alone in these challenges, they are universal for CEOs.

As someone who has seen both the good and the bad sides of sitting in the executive's chair, I can attest that *Lost at CEO* can help you avoid some of the common mistakes made by organization leaders. It provides a simple yet effective framework that can have an outsized impact on your organization.

Lost at CEO is an excellent book that provides a valuable roadmap for CEOs and business leaders. The storytelling is relatable, and the insights provided are actionable. I would highly recommend this book to anyone who wants to become a better leader and achieve their business goals. I think you'll enjoy it as much as I did, and I know you'll learn from it.

Find Your Focus and Do Great Things!

Trey Taylor,
Author, CEO, Taylor Insurance Services

Table of Contents

Introduction

Like with any book, there was risk in how I chose to tell this story.

If you're a CEO, executive, or just a business junkie like I am, chances are your bookshelf is already overrun with business books. You've read enough of them to know that this one is different by the time you make it to page 1.

Lost at CEO's strategic principles can be applied outside the traditional walls of business. Whether you are an educator, coach, parent, or leading a not-for-profit organization, these are valuable insights that will make you better in what you do and who you are.

This is indeed a "business" book in the sense that it discusses business. But it also bucks the mold that the vast majority of business books have been built with: be as straightforward and prescriptive as possible.

Do this. Do that. Here's the formula. Follow this five-step process. Each lesson is neatly categorized into its own chapter, then summarized to tell you exactly what to do next.

Unfortunately, that's not actually how business in the real world works. It doesn't happen by following a five-step process, and it definitely doesn't happen in neat little buckets. Being a leader is messy. It's stressful. And in the understatement of the year… *crap happens*. In writing this book, I wanted to capture that messiness in a way that felt real — in a way you could actually *feel* and relate to.

While so many of the "typical" business books out there can teach us a lot — and have even guided my own journey — there's also underrated value in people's *stories*.

That's why *Lost at CEO* isn't just a simple map explaining how to get from point A to point B. It won't be formulaic or prescriptive. It won't be dry advice laid out in list format. The lessons won't fit neatly into ten-page boxes. **Instead, you'll read a fictional story that traces a CEO's journey — in all its confusion, frustration, and, eventually, glory.**

I based much of this story on what I've learned over the past three-plus decades working directly with CEOs and other executives to scale organizations.

But Jack, our hero of the story, is not based on a single CEO. Rather, he's the composite of nearly *every* CEO I've met. He is the stressed-out entrepreneur running a multi-million-dollar company. He is hustling to get his business off the ground — but who is lost in the sea of day-to-day execution. He is the small-business CEO trying to manage a growing team and a chaotic market. He is the parent, the partner, the businessperson just trying to make something good in the world. He is all of us.

He is you.

In this story, Jack deals with the same frustrations, asks the same questions, and runs up against the same hurdles I've seen hundreds of executives deal with. But it's a rare group of leaders that eventually experience the same *triumphs* that Jack does.

This book maps out the process by which CEOs can finally reach that point. It's not a cookie-cutter recipe: You'll have to fill in the gaps according to *your* individual situation and company metrics. But these are the principles that the most successful CEOs use to move from *stuck* to *scaling*.

Most importantly, this story is not told from the perspective of some business owner who knows it all and is explaining all the answers to you from up high on a pedestal. This story is told from the perspective of someone still in the midst of *trying to figure it out*. The hero of our story is right in the thick of it. Just like you probably are right now.

And just like I have been.

I wrote this book in the margins of scaling my own business, 40 Strategy. I've written this story on airplanes as I travel to lead strategic retreats with clients. I've gotten words down between meetings. And there have been way too many days and nights, making voice memos while driving that I would later turn into actual chapters.

But I knew how important getting this content onto the page was. I've seen so many CEOs fizzle out, sell their companies at a loss, close up shop, and completely lose themselves (or their families) in the process of trying to scale an organization.

The best consulting firms in the world typically have only a 20 percent success rate of their clients adopting their strategic plan. The generally accepted strategic standard is that 90 percent of strategic plans fail. PwC has evidence that over *97 percent* of strategic plans fail.

It's my life's mission to end that trend.

I know the way forward *can* be different because I've seen it up close. I've been a part of seven different organizations that have successfully adopted their strategic plans to grow anywhere from 2x to 7x. I have applied and taught the principles you'll read about here within businesses and organizations — with extraordinary success.

And if you take what you learn from *Lost at CEO* and apply it to your organization, you can help me start a new trend in business:

You can be part of a new class of CEOs who scale the *right* way, still show up for their families, and help change the world for the better — one successful business at a time.

So it's time to stop just trying to keep your head above water.

It's time to captain your ship to its next-level destination.

Chapter 1

The Clock is Ticking

3:27 a.m. *Why can't I sleep?*

On a normal day, it wouldn't be uncommon to wake up at 5 a.m. or earlier. But this was Saturday — and a weekend getaway with my wife on top of that. Could my mind and body really not make it until at least 7 a.m.? *Apparently not.*

And God, could I use the rest.

Our weekend "getaway" got a late start, of course. I'd told Monica we could leave early Friday afternoon — but inevitably, I ended up in an unplanned meeting dealing with a customer dispute. And then had to make that "Sorry I'm late" call to Monica, who was patiently waiting. To be honest, she's gotten used to getting those calls.

"Jack," she'll usually say. "I love how hard you work. But I really just wish you were home more often."

I want that too. But this week, it just hasn't happened that way.

After I could finally extricate myself from the everyday hustle, I raced home and picked Monica up to drive to the beach, barely making our dinner reservation. But it was well worth the wait. She and I rarely get nights like this, where we can just relax (and I'm not cooped up in the office, or answering late-night calls).

Part of this trip is work-related, I guess: I'm scouting for potential places where my company, Stackflow, can host the upcoming strategic retreat. But it was a great excuse for Monica and me to drop off the kids at the in-laws' house and finally just *get away.*

3:56 a.m.: *Yet here I am, still awake in the middle of the night.*

It's not surprising to feel a little insomnia, though. Things haven't exactly been an easy road the past few years at Stackflow. We were barely able to scrape by after the devastating impact of COVID-19.

And then came the next big plague: inflation. I'd read about it from the 70s and 80s. But that was before *I* was the one making the decisions — and trying to navigate a company through the chaos.

Steel prices increased constantly. Plastic prices, too. But we couldn't just pass those prices on to our customers fast enough. There was no clear, obvious right decision. So most days? I was just trying to keep my head above water.

And then came the Great Resignation. It felt like every other day, someone was dropping into my office and saying, "You know, I just got this offer from the company down the street who says they're going to pay me double."

"Congratulations!" I would say, plastering a smile on. "That's amazing."

But on the other hand, I knew we were losing key wisdom and experience — just gone at a moment's notice. I was constantly afraid of who else would decide to walk out Stackflow's door.

All of this led to near record-low profits (even after increasing our sales by 20 percent).

Something had to give.

4:27 a.m.: *Enough complaining.*

Might as well get dressed, take a walk on the beach, and grab a coffee before scouting these strategic retreat locations.

Not that I have the tallest of expectations for what will come of this retreat. Let's be honest: the last three of them have yielded absolutely no results.

We had a great plan heading into 2020! (But we all know what happened then.) In 2021, there was still too much uncertainty to do much useful planning. And in 2022, we attempted a strategic plan — but I admit it was pretty half-hearted. Still too much uncertainty.

Even before all that external chaos, our strategic plans have rarely helped us make any real forward progress. We've hired outside consultants to help facilitate before. And we came up with some amazing ideas. Everyone at the company would feel excited about the plan — then drop right back into the reality of the day-to-day. We all got too busy with the daily work that we'd forget about the long-term strategic plan. I guess this is why most companies' strategic plans just end up collecting dust on some executive's bookcase.

But this year? This is going to be the year we finally build a strategy — and actually *execute* on it.

Because I know my clock is ticking.

5:13 a.m.: *This has to be the year I turn things around.*

I've had Stackflow for seven years now after a friendly acquisition. Those first few years looked pretty great, and we were even able to pay off a couple of the equity holders.

But after all the chaos of the last few years, the rest of the board is getting antsy. I can't blame them. Revenue is down, and we've got to find a way to get out of the hole.

That's what's brought me here today, to Seaside. I know time is running out, and we need an awesome strategy for the next year. And if we're going to craft a vision that everyone can get behind… Well, we need a great location to do the work from, right?

5:47 a.m.: *There's just something about the ocean waves coming in, day in and day out.*

Despite the peace of the beach, the ocean is relentless. Waves crash every ten seconds, slowly but consistently eroding the rocks into fine sand.

That's what it's felt like building Stackflow into what it is today. A continual grind. Some days, the work really has felt never-ending. There have been seasons where I've spent every day in the office, working long hours (and ignoring Monica in the process). It's taken a lot out of me and my relationships.

But I know things have to be different in this next season of growth. Just muscling through more work and staying at the office for longer hours isn't going to scale the company the way I need it to. (And that's not even accounting for all the external pressures of inflation, pandemic, labor shortages, supply chain drama… the list goes on.)

I look out at the ocean waves crashing onto the sand, and out toward the horizon. No other land in sight, just storm clouds brewing a little further west.

This year, we're going to need a plan that actually *works*. We're in uncharted waters, and I'm the sole person responsible for navigating us out of them — back to stable land.

Can we really use our time here in Seaside to draw up a strategy that will turn it all around?

Chapter 2

The Encounter

I can't answer that yet, especially before I've even had coffee. So I use the early-morning wake-up as a chance to head to the café, get my caffeine boost (and one to take back to Monica later), and clear my inbox. Unsurprisingly, it's overflowing. My email is like those waves, too: unrelenting.

It's only six in the morning, but there are already several people in line — including an average-size man close in age to me. He appeared to be a businessman (of some standing): nice loafers, crisp button-down shirt with the sleeves rolled halfway up, and a sporty Apple Watch on his wrist. He ordered a caramel latte with nonfat milk and sat down at one of the few open tables in the corner.

I grab my drink and open my laptop at the table beside his.

The man looks over: "Hello," he says.

I glance over, seeing the open book on the table.

"What are you reading over there?" I ask.

"Oh, just a book about business strategy," he says.

"Nice. I'm still struggling to even find time to read these days, with all the challenges going on in my business since COVID."

He nods in understanding.

"So do you come here to Seaside often?" he asks.

"Well, I used to, but I don't have as much time recently. I'm actually here partially for work. I'm scouting out a location for a strategic retreat soon."

"What a coincidence," the man laughs, gesturing to his book. "What do you plan on doing at the retreat? What kind of framework are you going to use?"

I pause in confusion. *Framework?* I ask myself. I had heard of balanced scorecards and OKRs and used SWOT from back in my Fortune 500 days. But it's hard to tell what he means.

"Well, we normally start out in SWOT — Strength, Weakness, Opportunity, Threat," I explain, in case this isn't the framework he's used to. "We'll probably brainstorm some ideas and flush out what we want to do by the end of the retreat. I really want to get everyone fired up this year to get it done."

"That's interesting," the man says, a look of inquisitiveness coming over his face. "But how does doing your SWOT analysis help you generate your strategic plan?"

Great question, I think to myself.

"Well, that's the way everyone does it," I say. "We try to use it as a brainstorming exercise and then try to come up with an action plan that addresses all the areas we talk about."

"So when you do that SWOT analysis, what type of research do you do?"

"We rarely even have that much time to do much research."

"I'm curious. Do you go through every single idea, or do you divide them according to priority?"

I laugh, thinking back to previous retreats, where everyone ends up on an hour-long tangent — and then the race to get back on track.

"Yeah, it always seems like we waste ninety-minute conversations about one unlikely opportunity or a remote threat in particular," I say. "But sometimes you just get a real black swan-like COVID. So, I guess it has been worth it."

"I know all about that," the man says. "So, how have your results been from your last strategic plan?"

"Well, it's messy," I laugh.

"You shouldn't feel bad," he replies. "I mean, 90 percent of strategic plans fail to even get two-thirds of their objectives done. You're not alone."

I pause, feeling at least a little better that it's clearly not just my company struggling.

"So, what are you in town for?" I ask. Enough about my company's failed strategic plans. *Trust me*, I think to myself. *I think about those almost every day.*

"I'm here for a strategy retreat too, actually," the man says. "But I'm coming at it from a different angle. I'm a consultant and I actually facilitate retreats for other companies."

"Now that's a cool coincidence," I say. "What have the results been?"

"Pretty solid! Our clients are usually in that 10 percent that actually follow through on their plans. Even during COVID, and all this inflation going on. Part of it is accountability too: We facilitate the retreat, but we work with them afterward to actually get it done."

At this point, I really start to question my own retreat ideas. Was it really going to be enough to (once again) go through a drawn-out SWOT analysis, brainstorm a ton of ideas, talk for hours about what we want to do… and then leave a retreat with no clear action plan for how we'd accomplish all those goals?

I could feel the beginning stages of a little déjà vu — but I know I want something different this year.

"Hey, any chance you're available in six weeks to help us on our retreat?" I ask, recognizing it's probably a long shot.

The man smiles.

"Thanks for the vote of confidence," he says. "But we're booked out for the next several months."

Speaking of strengths and weaknesses, I know one of mine is refusing to give up. And I'm not ready to let go of the idea of this man facilitating the kind of retreat that *actually* moves us forward as a company.

"I really want us to be successful, and I know I need help," I say. "Is there any other way I could get some guidance from you along the way?"

He glances down at his watch, then pulls out a card with his phone number and name on it. Charlie Joseph.

"I've got to head out soon, because we start here in 30 minutes," he says. "But give me a call in the future, and I'll see what I can do. I'm Charlie, by the way."

"Jack," I say, taking the card, and already making mental notes of the questions I want to ask.

As Charlie walks out of the café, I look down at my barely touched coffee. It isn't even warm anymore. And neither is my excitement for this upcoming retreat.

Chapter 3

Division

Three weeks later

In the end, I go with what I know: I book the retreat I already had planned. I send out the same SWOT analysis info to the team. I plan for the same general format as years past — against my better judgment. Charlie's advice about doing things a different way keeps ringing in my head. But I worry we're too close to the retreat date to really make wholesale changes to the format.

So I called him a few times over the next few weeks — eventually finally getting a 15-minute consult. I know I need guidance. I just have no idea where to start.

As Charlie picks up, I can hear the sound of people chattering in the background.

"Jack, thanks for the time today," Charlie says. "I'm about to board a flight, so we'll have to move quickly. What have you done so far to plan for the retreat?"

"Well, I booked the retreat center," I replied. "And I've asked everyone to fill out the SWOT analysis."

Even as it comes out of my mouth, I know it sounds lackluster. But that's why I'm on the phone with this consultant, I guess: to figure out what the heck comes next beyond that same strategic rut we've been in the past several years.

"Let me ask you this," Charlie says. "Have you asked yourself why you're doing this retreat? Why are you in business?"

"Well, we sell our products to our customers, of course. We want to make enough money to pay the staff's wages, have some profit-sharing when all goes well, and pay out some distributions to the owners."

"Okay," Charlie says. "So does that inspire you?"

I pause. To be honest, it really doesn't.

My silence over the phone speaks volumes.

"You don't have to be discouraged," Charlie says. "Most business owners fall into this trap. Just going after the next thing, and the next thing, and the next. Pushing for higher and higher revenues, but not really stopping to breathe and think about why they're actually doing what they do."

"I've just been so in the weeds," I say. "Every day feels like a mad dash just to keep our heads above water. I don't think I've even really thought about the 'why' in years."

"That's okay," Charlie says. "Here, let me email you the list of questions I take my clients through. These will really help you dial in on '*the why*' behind your business."

I can tell Charlie is used to moving fast, as by the time I open my laptop and navigate to my inbox, I can already hear the ping of his email coming in.

Why are you in business?
What is your purpose?
Where do you see yourself and your business in 10 years or more?
What's driving you to get there?
Why do we exist?
Why are we different from our competitors?
Why are employees compelled to stay?
What gets them excited to be here every day?
What's motivating them to make a difference?
How do you create value?

For your customers?
For your employees?
For your shareholders?
For you?

Reading through the questions, I realize how long it's been since I contemplated why we even came to work every day — beyond just manufacturing the products, making the sales, and paying the bills. And I have to admit, that sounded pretty boring compared to some of the early answers already floating through my brain as I scan through Charlie's list.

"The reality is, there are always going to be challenges," Charlie says, as the gate agent's voice comes over the speaker in the background. "There are always going to be excuses for why the company's performance is tanking. COVID, or a recession, or interest rates, or inflation. But you need to focus on what you can control. Focus back on your 'why.' Get together a detailed vision for why you're in business. When things get hard, this will be your North Star you'll keep navigating back to. Have your team start working on this now. It should be ready to go before you even get to the retreat."

I nod my head slowly, realizing how massively important this piece is — and how much we've been neglecting it at Stackflow.

"Think of this vision as a compass," Charlie says. "You need an alignment system that brings everyone together and keeps them rowing in the same direction. You don't want team members dropping anchors to hold you back because they're not aligned with your vision."

On the other end of the phone, I hear overhead bins being slammed shut.

"My plane's about to leave," Charlie confirms. "But let me know what you come up with."

I look down at my hastily scribbled notes.

I feel a little guilty for neglecting this kind of work for so long. We're here to actually make a difference. But it's obvious that's not really conveyed in the day-to-day structure of the business. Maybe that was partially why our company was struggling so much?

With a big sigh, I look up at my office door — and there are already two people waiting outside to talk to me. One of our sales guys is already rambling about yet another supply chain snag, about shipments being late, about price increases.

Here we go again.

Chapter 4

The Early Years

After seven years leading this business, I really thought I knew… well, *why* I was doing it. Why *we* were doing it.

On the day I officially became CEO, my excitement was off the charts. I'd put in nine years working for one of Stackflow's suppliers, but had finally reached an agreement to leave that company, purchase a stake in Stackflow, and move up to CEO.

And not without extensive effort: I had to pull money out of my IRA as a down payment, take out a line of credit from our home, get some financing from the bank, and team up with a couple of "friendly" investors.

It's an understatement to say this was a real source of stress at home. Monica just couldn't understand why I was leaving a wonderful job — with financial security — to take on this "risky" venture. Our three kids were young, and we had barely put aside enough to fund their college educations.

Now, I was putting us all at risk. Their futures. Our home. What little retirement we had.

And for what? To become CEO?

I was risking the barely-one-semester of college funds that we saved in a 529 plan. Perhaps community college wasn't such a bad idea for the kids?

But this was important. I wanted to provide them a better opportunity.

The job came with higher compensation, of course — but only after we returned the company to profitability and paid down the debts. The end goal was to get the company back to that point, sell it, and easily replenish our retirement and education funds (and ideally put them a few years ahead of schedule). The whole plan would put me in a position to choose my next adventure with comfort — whatever that opportunity may be.

To ease Monica's mind, I called up an old CPA friend to create some financial models to show her how we could return the company to its previous profitability — and more than double our own money.

It didn't seem outside the realm of reality. I knew the previous owner had stopped investing in the company a while ago, and seemed more interested in playing golf and duck hunting than running a company.

But that wasn't me. I knew I could turn things around there — and reap the rewards in a few years. Plus, my golf game was mediocre, and I hadn't shot a gun in years.

"Monica," I told her. "This is an easy decision."

After all the financial models, an independent valuation, and, yes, a trip to the beach and the spa that I threw in for her, Monica finally came around. She trusted me — and I knew I couldn't let her, or our kids, down.

So I made the deal.

And even though I'd preached patience to my wife and had convinced her to have faith, cutting that check still felt like one of the scariest decisions of my life. I'd never held that amount of money in my hand. I had to knock myself out of the habit of checking my retirement account, because — well, there was hardly anything there anymore. The sinking feeling in my gut never really went away.

But on the surface, it was all smiles and handshakes. I was outwardly confident — and knew I could do things better than the duck-hunting previous owner. I just needed a chance. And after 15 years, I finally had it.

Within weeks, I completely stopped checking that retirement account. How would I have had the time anyway? Like a dive into the deep end of the pool, I was immediately engulfed in running the business.

The hours were long, the stress was accelerating, and very quickly, the doubts started creeping in. My wife stopped counting the number of dinners I missed and the times I walked into the front door late — again.

Sixty days into the acquisition, I thought to myself, "What in the Sam Hill have I gotten myself into?"

The employees seemed afraid to make the big changes I knew we needed. Their work habits were awful. Our manufacturing tools were aging. Computers were out-of-date. The sales strategy seemed to be something along the lines of "Build it, and they will come." This concept may play well in movies — but in a business setting? Not so much.

The hits just kept coming.

One of our biggest customers was a golfing buddy with the previous owner. When I took over, he decided it would be best for him to retire as well.

The supplier where I'd put in nearly a decade of work — a decade of successes, relationships, birthdays, blood, sweat, and tears — decided to pull the rug out from under our feet too. I knew they'd been unhappy I had left, but thought they would understand. Apparently not. Within a year of my move to CEO, my old company decided to stop providing the core product that Stackflow had been using for 12 years.

They said it was a business decision, a chance to focus on new markets, a chance at higher profit margins. All the usual excuses. But I knew better.

All of that, of course, led to our current mode: panic.

We found a new supplier for the core component, which was great. But we had to settle for a larger distribution company, where we never seemed to be able to get the same service and priority as we'd had at our previous distributor. Here, we were just another account of thousands, with a rotating account manager from the state university who knew nothing about our business or our needs. He could barely remember our names.

So I did what I do best: work hard. Develop relationships with customers, suppliers, and employees. Maximize sales. Manage costs. Bring cash to the bottom line. Reinvest. Do it all over again.

It paid off: over the next three years, I transformed Stackflow from an unknown commodity into a competent leader. Sales grew 12 percent annually. Bottom line went up 8 percent. We managed our banking relationships and paid our debts. We paid our first profit share plan in seven years. When I delivered a profit share check to Lisa, a long-time warehouse employee, she cried. It was the first time she'd had enough money to take her family on a one-week vacation to Disney.

The board was happy, employees were happy, I was happy.

It's not rocket science, after all.

Until it is.

I was averaging 55 to 70 hours of work a week, not even including travel time. It seemed like every other week, I was on another plane, visiting a customer or another supplier or a trade show (sometimes all at once).

And don't forget the three-hour dinners to schmooze the people who needed schmoozing. I was an all-league quarterback in high school — but these days? I look more like an offensive lineman.

With all the stress over the past few years — of working overtime to turn this ship around — my marriage had suffered. Monica is constantly telling me we need to have more date nights. But those rarely happen. I make it to some of the kids' events, but those usually come as a pleasant surprise rather than an expectation.

And no matter what, I have to admit: I'm rarely present. There's always a worry at the back (or front, really) of my mind: a customer order, the latest employee threatening to leave, rising costs. If I had a dollar for every time one of my kids has gotten right up in my face to ask, "Dad? Did you hear me?" — well, maybe I wouldn't have to worry so much about all those increasing costs.

And that was before everything REALLY fell apart.

Chapter 5

The Tsunami

March 2020.

I could go the rest of my life without talking or thinking about COVID. Every CEO I know feels the same. But it's impossible to overstate just how much it impacted our company.

The pandemic hit Stackflow hard, to say the least. Initially, our customers stopped answering the phone. Then they canceled purchase orders. If not for the PPP loan, Stackflow might not have survived.

I mean, we make things — it's not like we could press a button on our laptops and make our physical products manufacture themselves. I felt like I had a duty to be there alongside my team at the plant, so I showed up to the office every day. That's leadership.

Still, we lost employees during the Great Resignation. I had to bump up wages to attract people back to work. Our production labor team went from $13/hour to $22/hour on average. And that was just one part of the domino effect. COVID kept sending shock waves into the supply chain. Smaller companies like us had to fight to get any products we could. Higher demand over a short supply raised prices. Again. And again. And again. To make the same gross product margin, we had to increase our prices multiple times, and we still have not returned to our previous gross margins.

For any company that made it through COVID, the reward was an economy that had completely shifted beneath their feet. *(Congratulations!)*

So, we survived. But we were always playing catch-up. Our costs would increase, and we'd still have open sales orders at the old prices. We changed our sales order terms from 180-day pricing to sometimes 30 days or less. The market was so volatile that certain vendors would only provide spot prices.

We bumped our prices to double-digit percentages — and our veteran sales team couldn't seem to understand why we had to make such substantial changes. Usually, this meant they'd cave during negotiations. Yet another hit to our margins.

I spent about 18 months, if not more, with a giant hole in my gut. We increased revenue by 32% from 2019 — but the reality was, we were making less money today. We were shipping the same number of products we had before; the only difference was inflation.

Internally, no one was doing better at their work. And things seemed like they kept getting worse.

Fast-forward to now, and I have to laugh a little. It's hard to even peel back the layers of what's happened since 2020 — much less unravel our "why" as a company from all the chaos. What CEO has time to think through those things when there are bigger, more urgent priorities?

Do I try to raise prices again? Will they work in this economy? Do I lay off more staff? After everything they've put into the company since the pandemic began? Do I go offshore? Do I automate? What's the right approach?

Not to mention, the value of the company has tanked. It's worth less today than when I bought it originally.

My whole goal from the start was to grow Stackflow, sell it, and provide for my family's college educations, retirement, and extra cash in the bank. Oh, and we had already upgraded our house too — our mortgage is double what it used to be.

I feel like a failure. And I'm not sure how much some consultant I met at Starbucks is going to help with that. Still, I want to give his method a shot. Because I'm quickly realizing mine (and our team's) isn't going to cut it.

Chapter 6

Survivor Night

Wednesday night. *Survivor* night. It's one of Monica's favorite shows, and I try my best to make it to the couch in time to watch it with her. Lately, it's been a struggle to even get through the front door by the time it's over, and she's already ready for bed.

But tonight, I'm here — with my laptop open, sure. But I'm physically here.

The team has already started sending me their SWOT analysis answers, and I scroll through the documents.

But first, a scene grabs my attention. A woman with a prosthetic leg is struggling to get through an obstacle to win this competition to "earn immunity" for a week. Her prosthetic leg is literally slipping off due to the humid conditions. But she keeps trying. The rest of the competitors are way ahead of her. But she doesn't quit. She falls — again, and again, and again. But she finally restores her balance and confidence. The last part of the competition is throwing a ball through a hoop. She finally catches up, and now everyone is equal. As everyone else struggles to make the shot, she drains the shot in her first attempt. She cries, and her competition is now admiring her character and grit. My wife has tears in her eyes. I find myself caught up with emotion too — and inspiration.

After composing myself, I look back at the computer screen. *Not quite as inspiring.*

Everyone's answers are pretty consistent from the past few years. No new or innovative ideas. I have to stop myself from rolling my eyes at the same tired answers. This feels more like the *Survivor* lady at the beginning of the obstacle. Where is the hope?

It's not the only area of the business that's getting a little stale. Every time I sit down for a meeting with the board, it's like I get the same questions over and over again. Sometimes I wonder if they've even reviewed the packet that we spend all week preparing.

Then it's a lot of rinse-and-repeat from previous meetings: "How is your sales team?" "How is the marketing process?" "Have you considered using Google Ads?" "Do you have the right colors for your brand?" "Can you update the words in the board minutes? They seem a little off." "Could you make sure that you have the cover sheet on the TPS report?" That movie reference from *Office Space* always makes me chuckle. Monica, still engaged in Survivor, gives me a strange glance, wondering what I'm laughing about.

But most importantly, I always hear from the board: "When are you going to get profits back up?"

Needless to say, my "friendly" investors are starting to get a little less friendly. Some of their other investments haven't fared well in this new economy, and everyone's 401(k) is down with the stock market. Everybody is on edge — and I can't blame them.

But figuring out how to turn things around for them? It's going to require a fresher approach than the ones I'm flipping through on my computer now.

Like most other CEOs I know, it's hard to find anyone to bounce ideas off of. Sure, I have my team — but they're rarely fully aware of all the pressures (internal and external) on the C-suite. I have my monthly business mastermind group — a great group of other business owners in the same range of revenue. But in that kind of roundtable setup, I'm lucky to get five or ten minutes to discuss my specific problems. Sometimes we all just jump on the call and spend the time complaining about the issues that have come across our desks — which can be cathartic. People think it's all sunshine in the C-suite, so it's hard to find people who really *get* what we go through. But sometimes that commiseration can feel more like a counseling session than a business meeting. And I'm not looking for counseling, or inspirational quotes. I need answers.

My wife looks over at me again as I heave a deep sigh. I'm pulling up each team member's SWOT document on my computer, and getting more and more frustrated. No one seems to be stepping outside the rut that we've already dug ourselves into the past few years. It's the same old answers, reframed within the context of this year.

Our controller, Mark, has the same "strategy" he always does: cut costs.

In operations, Mike lists our strengths as just "getting it done." And he *does* get it done, admirably. He puts in 60 hours a week already. But leaning on that doesn't feel like a sustainable strategy for scaled growth.

I click over to a few more documents and sigh again. There's literally no one I can trust in the company to tell the truth. And there's no one I can really talk to about how worried I am about the future.

My whole team thinks I have it all figured out — and I've honestly never been so uncertain before. If I share that vulnerability, I'm at risk of appearing weak and killing the team's confidence in me. But not talking to anyone about all this is beginning to weigh on me too.

I finally shut my laptop and reach for the TV remote to turn up the volume. Tribal council is starting, and I want to tune in at least for the end of the episode.

At the back of my mind, I'm still mucking through all those stale ideas I just read, and feeling anxious about how any of them are actually going to move us forward. Because designing a strategy that actually turns this company around? Getting the whole team rowing in the same direction?

The company felt more like the real game of *Survivor*. And I didn't want to get voted off the island. We need that hero that survives the obstacle. Who is it going to be?

I make a note in my calendar to give Charlie another call in the morning. He really might be the last remaining person who can help.

Chapter 7

Changing Course

"Hey Jack, I'm stuck in the car for the next 45 minutes," Charlie says as soon as he picks up the phone. "I'm on my way from the airport in Dallas to a client's office. So we've got some time."

I spent the first few minutes getting Charlie up to speed: We did the SWOT analysis. Got effectively the same information we have every other year. Our bottom line isn't looking good. And our team is about to be in for a surprise when there's no profit-sharing at the end of this year. (Ironic, considering we just had to pay our salespeople record commissions, which isn't exactly helping the bottom line.)

I've never had a problem paying people for doing excellent work. But paying record commissions when the company is losing money makes no sense.

For 25 minutes, I complain about everything going wrong. The list doesn't seem to be getting any shorter. By the time I get it all off my chest, I realize I'm halfway into my time with Charlie — and he'll be getting out of the car in 20 minutes.

"What do I need to do next?" I ask halfheartedly.

"Jack, where are you going?"

"What do you mean, where am I going? I'm going broke if I continue this. I might lose everything."

I said it with such emotion that I almost had to hold back tears. *Where did that come from?*

"Jack, I hear you. This is a challenging time. That's true for every CEO I work with, so you're not alone. But to get different results, you have to do things differently. Let's zoom out: What does your company look like in ten years or more?"

This catches me off guard. I'm just trying to keep cash flow steady, and he's asking me questions about the next decade?

Charlie seems to sense some of my skepticism.

"Jack, I'm serious," he says. "What are your long-term hopes and dreams? When all you're worried about is bailing water out of your boat, you're basically drifting around in a vast ocean. Right now, you have no lighthouse in sight. We need to create that light so you have something to steer toward. And once you have a destination in mind, you can start drawing a map to get there. You have to develop a new vision. Otherwise, what are you even navigating toward?"

I can see his point.

A half-dozen more questions sprang to mind, but I could already hear Charlie's car stopping in the background.

"Here's the next step," Charlie says. "Tell me what your business looks like in ten years. Where will you be? What products and services are you delivering? What are your clients saying about you? What does your team look like? How engaged is your team?"

"Do this in the next 48 hours," he continues. "Send it to me in two days, and I'll look over it on my next flight."

"Is there a format I should use?" I ask

"That doesn't matter right now," he says. "Just spend the next two days rethinking what your future will look like. Don't worry about the 'how' yet — just focus on the what and the why. Who will you be? Get down as much detail as you can. Try to set some bigger goals you believe you have at least a 51 percent chance of reaching. So, a stretch, but still possible. I'm excited to see what you come up with."

In the background, Charlie's car door slams, and I set my phone back on the desk.

Forty-eight hours, I think to myself.

I'm on the clock now.

Chapter 8

The Future

6:03 a.m.: This is really the only time I have to work on things outside the day-to-day execution of keeping the company afloat. If it doesn't get done at the crack of dawn, it's probably not going to get done. So before my inbox starts really rolling, I get to the local coffee shop as soon as it opens, grab my favorite caramel latte and a bagel, then sit at a booth over in the corner. I take out a fresh notebook and turn to a blank sheet.

What does our future look like in ten years or more?

Well, I will be 56 years old in one decade. I pause. *Wow, I am getting older.*

I would need my retirement figured out by then. Who even knows if Social Security will still be around by that point? Not to mention, Social Security would barely cover our basic needs, let alone visiting grandkids or doing all the traveling Monica wants to do. We've certainly put off enough vacations already — retirement is supposed to be when we can finally start saying "yes" to that trip to Italy.

Still, 56 isn't as long away as I once thought. And who knows what kind of state my health will be in then? My back problems are only getting worse, especially with the physical shape I'm in. By the time I get to retirement, will I even have the energy and drive to enjoy it?

Something clicks into place in my head: I'd better figure out how to turn this company around. Otherwise, I'm not going to be able to enjoy my retirement the way I've always dreamed. Heck, I might not even be able to retire at all.

A new sense of urgency replaces my initial skepticism about Charlie's assignment. I'm starting to see why he has me doing this process before diving into P&L sheets or strategy planning.

Riding the wave of that momentum, I write page after page after page in my notebook — an hour and a half with my pen practically floating across the paper. I hadn't thought this deeply about the company's future since I bought it. And frankly, at that point, it just felt like a transaction.

Now, it feels like so much more.

I take one last sip of my latte and look down at what I've come up with: the entire future of Stackflow, broken down into six sections, and written as if everything had *already happened* (a trick Charlie suggested).

- **Employees:** *We've built a place where people WANT to come to work (and that's proven by the extensive list of applicants we receive every time there's an opening). We have a combination of veterans and new employees providing fresh energy — but everyone is highly skilled and well-trained. There are promotional opportunities, and 10 percent of every employee's time is focused on innovation and idea generation. Our team is highly engaged, and everyone knows that the work they do actually contributes to the overall health of the company. They understand why they do what they do, and it makes them highly engaged. With regular open forums and collaboration, everyone feels like they have a voice.*

  Plus, everyone's happy because profit-sharing is back. The whole team has gotten payouts in 11 of the past 12 quarters. In the day-to-day, employees get to enjoy a newly renovated office space — which is practical enough to get the job done, but luxurious enough to provide a real "wow" experience. So much so that employees' friends, families, and significant others often come by the office for lunch.

- **Customers:** *We genuinely care about our clients and want to provide them with a "red carpet" experience — all the way from initial contact, to support from our sales team, to delivering high-quality products on time, and unmatched customer service all the way through. Our product guarantee sets us apart from the competition, and our clients trust we'll follow through on our word. Because of all that, our Net Promoter Score rivals some of the best companies in the world.*

- **Suppliers and partners:** *After all the supply chain chaos of the COVID days, we knew we needed to buckle down on this part of the business. We now have a trusted supply chain network and service providers. The flow of products to our customers in the U.S. (and abroad) is constant. And we just opened up a new distribution office on the other side of the country, so we can stay competitive with freight. We've consolidated all our manufacturing within the Americas, and have fully embraced a leaner philosophy across the whole enterprise: efficient operations, the right amount of inventory, and a clean setting. Everything runs like a well-oiled machine.*

- **Shareholders:** *Four years ago, we generated a liquidity event to pay previous shareholders a 3X return on their original purchase price. Today, we're evaluating offers from a new buyer group — who are interested in how much value we've been able to add since the previous acquisition. Better yet, our board meetings actually create value now: they're clear, crisp, and to the point. There's time for thoughtful discussion, and all the key members participate in our strategic planning process.*

- **Management team:** *Leadership is at an all-time best at Stackflow. We've brought on a COO, CFO, and CRO who have all scaled companies in the past to the size we're now shooting for. They all have strong incentive programs to keep them motivated, and the autonomy to run their respective operations within the overall umbrella of our strategic plan.*

  Outside the C-suite, our second-level management group is top-notch. They're not only great operators and managers, but they understand constant change must happen if we're going to continue to lead the market. They're not afraid of that change — they embrace it, and are always ready to lead their teams in pursuing it.

- **CEO:** *I've finally extricated myself from most of the day-to-day execution, and am back to being a true strategic leader and mentor for all our other leaders. I meet with customers and suppliers at key regional events to develop relationships and figure out how Stackflow can keep improving. Soon enough, I'm even going to migrate out of that role. We're preparing to promote our COO to CEO, and I plan to move to a chairperson position — so I can be even further away from day-to-day operations.*

  Sure, I still work. But I take plenty of time off these days. My family and I just finished a two-week trip to Italy, Greece, and Croatia. My relationship with Monica is better than it's ever been. Unless I'm traveling (which I'm doing even less of now), I'm always open for dinner. And I haven't missed a kid's sporting event in more than three years. My health is better than it was even 20 years ago, and I just finished my fourth half-marathon.

  I have a close network of friends and other business leaders that I can tap into for support, brainstorming, or just some commiseration (because there will never be a true end to the challenges of being CEO). I still invest in myself, through mentors and coaches — because now that my hands aren't tied by day-to-day execution, I can really focus on being my best.

I'm back to feeling successful — and most importantly, I'm happy.

I finish writing that last line with a flourish of the pen — and notice tears welling up in my eyes. Wow. That surprises me. But this feels right.

"But how on earth are we supposed to get there?!" I can't help but think to myself.

As I look up, I'm surprised to see the coffee shop filled with the morning rush of customers. I've been so engaged that I hadn't even noticed anyone else coming in.

And I hadn't paid attention to my phone, either. I swipe it back off airplane mode to see what the damage is: three missed calls, two voicemails, and five text messages.

Could be worse, I sigh to myself.

Well… until I read one of the texts from Mark, the Stackflow controller.

"Hi Jack," it reads. "I called and left you a message. Northing, our largest customer, is threatening to leave us."

Son of a gun.

I quickly pack up my bag and rush outside to my car. As I speed into the fast lane of the interstate, I have the same thought I have, at some point, almost every day: *Time to survey the damage.*

Chapter 9

Customer Success?

One week later

One unscheduled trip to Northing's head office, one exceptionally long dinner, three glasses of wine each at said dinner, and a lot of schmoozing later, I finally start to breathe again. The folks at Northing seemed to have finally calmed down — but not without me providing more concessions than I would have liked.

They'd been unhappy with the recent price increases (who wouldn't be?). But add those increases to inconsistent (read: late) deliveries, and I couldn't blame them for their frustration. One of our key competitors was offering lower prices, plus the promise of on-time deliveries.

To save the relationship, I committed to no more price increases for at least 12 months unless we saw another significant rise in commodity prices. Plus, we would put an end to our freight surcharges. I threw in a 2 percent discount if our products were late.

All that compromise — plus the steak dinner and bottle of Bordeaux at his favorite restaurant — seemed to keep disaster at bay. At least for now.

I step onto the plane the next morning, still feeling the effects from that extra glass of wine — and those extra concessions.

How much are we actually making from Northing? I wonder to myself as I stow my bag in the overhead bin and take my seat.

I think back to the beginning of our relationship with Northing. They were one of the first big customers I helped our VP of Sales win when I first arrived at Stackflow. It was steady business — and even accounted for a quarter of our revenue at its peak. That had moved back down to 15 percent, thankfully. But that didn't take away the sinking feeling in my gut every time I thought about the possibility of losing their business.

Then again, they're impossible to work with: always changing specs after the purchase order, for one. Plus, we had to hold so much inventory to meet their demand — probably $500K at this point. Sometimes I wonder if we make any money at all from Northing.

As we reach cruising altitude on the flight back home, I pull out my computer and navigate to the vision document I created last week. Because of all the chaos with Northing, I haven't even had a chance to look at it again since my coffee shop writing session.

As I scroll through the sentences that had me so excited last week, I realize this is a document that's not going to do a lot of good just stored on my computer. I need to share this with the whole leadership team. I need to get people on the boat. And if they don't want to get on the boat and help me row toward this end destination, I probably need to make personnel changes too.

I get to the bottom of the page, where I've outlined the "CEO" portion of the vision. Well, the management team probably doesn't need to read *this* part.

As I read through my ten-year CEO dreams, I feel a tug of frustration. This week has been practically the opposite of what I have written here. I'm rushing around trying to save a client relationship, the company's future is still very much at stake, and I'm missing yet another Friday night with my family. My son's basketball team is playing a rival team tonight, and I'll be lucky if I even make it to the court by the fourth quarter.

This definitely wasn't the first time I'd had to rush to an expensive steak dinner with Northing's head honchos, and in the process, miss a kid's sporting event. When I returned home, my bloodshot eyes would be met by Monica's disapproving eyes — a look I've seen way too often over the past few years. Who could blame her for being mad?

I look out the window, past the plane's wing, and to the puffy clouds that we're jutting through. Far from feeling like a successful business trip, this trip just felt like a band-aid over a gaping wound. We still haven't figured out how to turn the business around. And I have some serious doubts that *this* — running ourselves ragged to chase a high-maintenance customer — was the sustainable way to actually get ourselves out of the hole.

There has to be a better way. And I'm close to discovering it.

Chapter 10

Getting in the Same Boat

As I come down from the adrenaline of the last-minute rush to save Northing, and — spurred by the motivation for that kind of chaos to never happen again — I come back to work more excited than I've been in a long time.

With my vision in hand (and in my head), I finally feel a little hope. We can dig ourselves out of this hole. We can find a way to be profitable again.

But I know I need the whole team's help to make it happen. They need to buy into this vision as much as I have.

I get back to work on Monday, and our next management team meeting is scheduled for 10 a.m. Usually this is the space where we just complain about the week. But I decided to hijack the hour this time around. It's time to get our leadership team's input on this vision. Before everyone walks into the conference room, I distribute copies of the vision document and set one in front of each place at the table.

"This is just a draft," I say as everyone arrives and sits down. "But I've been working to nail down some pieces of the Stackflow vision moving forward. I want you to read through this document and start thinking through what you would add or modify."

Mark, the controller, is the first to speak up.

"Wow, you've really put a lot of time in this," he says. "Things have been really challenging lately, and I appreciate you thinking about the future. I know I've been wondering all this myself. So if these are the goals, how do we get there?"

"Don't worry about the 'hows' just yet," I responded. "It's important to just focus on *what* we want to shoot for the long-term. We'll dig into the 'hows' afterward, when we land on a shared vision everyone can feel excited about. Let's spend this time stretching and thinking about what could be possible."

Nancy, our marketing manager, grabs a whiteboard and some markers to start writing down ideas.

I'm amazed at how fast the time goes. This is the most engaged I've seen the leadership team in one of our weekly meetings and I don't even know how long. Everyone is contributing. And the ideas are actually exciting — not just the same old, same old that we're all used to. There are ideas for new positions to create, a potential new service line, some changes we could make to our machinery, and a lot more.

By the time I look down at my watch and see that we've gone over our allotted hour, I'm fired up. And I can tell that the people around me at the table are too. But I know we can't get too carried away just yet: there's still day-to-day work to be done.

"Let's table this until tomorrow," I say, gesturing up to the clock on the wall. "Write down all your comments or ideas. We'll set another meeting for tomorrow to go over everything and finalize the vision."

To my mild surprise, every member of the management team shows up to the next meeting with their own pages of notes. In two hours, we make more progress than we'd made in entire days' worth of strategic retreats in previous years. We're efficient with our time, the ideas are flowing, and the time flies yet again.

Maybe there really is something to Charlie's whole visioning process, I think to myself.

When we finish up, I give marching orders for the next step.

"Gather a handful of people from each of your departments and meet with them to discuss what we came up with here," I say. "Ask them for their own long-term vision. If there's something they think we should pursue, or if they have opinions about what we have here, really take the time to listen to what they have to say. It's important we get everyone on board if we're going to make this work."

Everyone starts shuffling papers around and gathering their things to leave the meeting. It feels like I have electricity moving through my bloodstream. I'm so excited about the long-term vision that we've come up with — even the "stretch" ones that we may only have a 51 percent chance of reaching.

But that's the threshold Charlie told us to shoot for. I'm trusting the process. And I know it's time to start getting everyone in the boat — so we can all row together toward those destinations.

If only I knew that one of the first people to jump overboard was going to be somebody in that very room.

Chapter 11

Vision to Value

A knock at my door.

I glance up and see Julie, one of our production managers, standing in the doorway.

"Hi, Julie," I say. "What's up?"

She shuffles her feet a little and purses her lips. Whatever she's about to say, she's nervous to spill.

"I'm not really sure what all is going on with this vision thing you're doing," she says. "But I felt like I needed to say this. Mike has been calling you out about it. He thinks you're setting goals that aren't even possible. He just kind of forced us to go through the exercise with him, but the whole time, he was talking about how it was kind of pointless. I think it sounds pretty cool, but I just wanted to let you know it seems like not everybody is on board with it."

I try to hide the frustration on my face.

Mike, our operations manager, had been in that conference room with the rest of us. He'd seen all the ideas coming to life on the whiteboard. Why is he throwing me under the bus like this now? And why doesn't he want a clear-cut mission and an exciting vision to work toward? That's to the benefit of him and his team, too.

"Well, thanks for telling me, Julie," I say. "I really appreciate you stepping up and saying something."

She nods and heads back to her cubicle. I know it probably wasn't easy for her to come into the CEO's office like that and speak up about her direct boss.

But now what?

I don't want to bring up my conversation with Julie to Mike, because he doesn't need to know she was the one who said something. But at the same time, I need to find a way to address this.

Stuck in the middle and not sure which direction to head, I do the first thing that pops to mind: text Charlie.

"Do you have a few minutes for a phone call?" I type out.

"Even better," Charlie responds within a few seconds. "I just wrapped a client meeting down the street from your office. Meet for coffee in 15?"

I arrive at the coffee shop, and Charlie is already sitting in a corner booth. Quite the stroke of luck that he's in the same general office park today, because I could use his advice on this one.

As I sit down with my latte, I take him through everything that's happened throughout the visioning process. The work I did on my own, the whiteboards and management input, the conversation with Julie. The betrayal by Mike.

"You should embrace this as a positive," Charlie says after I finish.

I frown and take a sip of my coffee. I find it hard to believe that one of my key leaders throwing me under the bus to his team is a step in the right direction.

"You'll definitely want to address it," Charlie quickly says when he sees the look on my face. "But getting clear on your vision means that this kind of stuff will bubble to the surface a lot easier. It makes your decision-making even more powerful. Keep in mind, some people don't want to have to make changes. They like exactly where they're at. They like the power they currently have. Or at least they *feel* like they're in control. But this is all a long-term process, and sometimes it takes people more time to get on board with changes you want to make. It just means you're growing and evolving. If you didn't have reactions like this come up at the start of this process, I'd say you're aiming too low or too easy with your visioning process."

That's an interesting way to think about it. It makes sense that the higher we shoot, the more people we're going to leave behind.

"Have you ever done anything with your team to evaluate their strengths and talents?" Charlie asks.

I flash back to those old personality assessments I made everyone take about five years ago. I shudder a little, because I remember how much everyone hated them — and how little those assessments actually did for us in the long run.

Trying to hide my skepticism, I tell Charlie I don't put much stock in that kind of stuff.

"Yeah, I understand," Charlie says. "We just need to level up a little from those kinds of assessments. The real difference is we're not measuring people's personalities. We're evaluating what they're good at — their talents — and then matching their job duties with those strengths. And vice versa. If they have certain weaknesses, then you probably don't need to hand them the reins on those kinds of responsibilities."

"Hmm," I reply. "What do you mean?"

"Have you ever noticed giving the same type of project to the same person… and it never seems to get done?"

The budget, I immediately think. I can't even count the number of times I've handed over that responsibility to Mark — or the number of times I have to follow up to make sure it's actually getting done. The time I spend reminding him to do it, I could probably have just used to do it myself.

When I explain the situation to Charlie, he nods immediately in understanding.

"I can make some guesses right now," he says. "I'd guess that budgeting isn't part of Mark's strengths. And when something isn't in someone's wheelhouse like that — well, things just don't get done. Not to mention, employee satisfaction and engagement are going to be pretty low."

I try to remember how responsibility for the budget got passed onto Mark in the first place. Did we ever stop to think about whether he would actually be good at it, or did we just hand it over because there was no one else to do it?

"So here's my suggestion," Charlie says. "Before your strategic retreat — that's coming up in a few weeks, right? — do a strengths' assessment for each of your employees before you all show up for the meeting. Send it to me, and I'll take a quick look to give you my two cents. This will help you see everyone's talents, and how you can use them. This is going to be incredibly important for the whole process of planning and execution. You want to be able to rely on the right people for the right jobs that they're naturally good at."

"By the way," he continues. "Have you decided your agenda for the retreat yet?"

Yet another thing on my to-do list, I think.

"I have kind of the standard agenda that we've done every other year," I reply. "But based on everything that's happened, I think we probably need to change it. What do you recommend?"

"Well, I have a seven-step process I usually take my clients through," Charlie says. "You've already started the first one, and that's establishing your vision. That way you're aligning everyone and getting the whole team in the same boat. The next step is figuring out where you're actually going."

"Seems pretty important," I say facetiously.

He nods enthusiastically.

"This is one of the most important distinctions most business owners don't understand. There's a difference between your vision and your *destinations*."

I lean in, as if he's about to tell me the greatest secret to business success in the history of the world. (Heck, maybe he is.)

"Your vision describes what it looks like to arrive in the future," Charlie says. "You know your vision is working when people begin to formulate in their own minds how they see themselves within that future. For others, it'll be a great point of clarity, because they actually *don't* see themselves in that future — and that can be a sign for them to leave. You want everyone on one ship. And ideally, you want them to *choose* to be on that ship."

"That definitely makes sense," I say. "But how do destinations differ from what I've already done? Isn't the vision just listing out where we want to go?"

"Yes and no," Charlie says. "The vision is all about where you want the ship to go in the long run. It's like the compass you use to navigate, or the North Star you look up to make sure you're headed in the right direction. A destination is an exact place the ship is *going* to end up along the way, within a certain timeframe. Think of it like a port or a harbor."

This is starting to make sense in my head. I could envision my team and I all on the same ship, stopping at port after port, on the way to the end vision.

"So a destination is kind of like the goals you set on the way to the overall vision," I say.

"Kind of," Charlie says. "But I hate using the term 'goal.' The problem with leaders saying they have a goal of getting somewhere is that most goals fail miserably. Here, take a look at this study."

Charlie pulls out his phone and navigates to an article he already has bookmarked. (*Of course he does*, I think to myself.) It's a study from the University of Scranton that says people fail their New Year's goals 92 percent of the time.

"I don't know about you," Charlie says. "But I don't even want to use language that's associated with consistent failure. So that's why I never tell my clients to set goals. Still, we need language to talk about the smaller steps along the way toward a vision. We still need a way to break down our ten-year vision into three-year and one-year stepping stones."

"Think of it this way," he continues. "How often do you hear of a cruise ship never reaching its destination? How about an airplane? If the plane doesn't reach its destination, it's newsworthy. Something like 80 to 90 percent of airplanes not only reach their destinations; but they get there on time. This is how we want to view your one-year destinations — or goals, as you put it."

I think back to my last flight, from the meeting with Northing in Dallas, back to Portland. That two-hour delay had been a pain — but I did eventually reach my destination. And it was one of the few times this year that I hadn't arrived at my destination within the timeframe I expected. More often than not, I could count on the airline to get me where I needed to go, when I needed to be there.

I want that same confidence at Stackflow.

"When it comes to setting your destinations, I like to focus on one-year and three-year timelines," Charlie explains. "Some companies might use five-year timelines if they're bigger or have a different life cycle. But for most organizations under 250 employees, one-year and three-year timelines work really well."

"So how do you know which goals… sorry, *destinations,* you should set within a one-year timeframe and which ones should be within three years?" I ask.

"A one-year destination should be set with a high sense of confidence. It should have about a 90 percent likelihood of success, with the right people, processes, and systems in place. Notice I didn't say 100 percent. There's always risk. There are always unknowns. Nobody's perfect. Our planning could go wrong. We could get hit with an unexpected storm, like a pandemic. Or maybe government regulations change an industry overnight. You already know that in 2020, most organizations' strategic plans had to be thrown out. But in general, your one-year destinations should have a strong possibility of happening."

The chatter of the coffee shop fades away as I race to scribble down notes. This is a whole new way of thinking about goal-setting than I've ever experienced. And I know it has the power to potentially completely shift momentum at Stackflow.

"Just remember not to go too soft on setting these destinations," Charlie says.

"Too soft?" I look up from my notebook page. "What do you mean?"

"Let's say an organization wants to grow 5 percent — from $10 million to $10.5 million year over year," Charlie says. "Let's say this is a classic 'sandbag' plan. The team has super high confidence that they'll reach that destination before the year even ends. Internally, the team even believes they could hit $11 million or higher."

"But then they set the threshold for company bonuses at $10.5 million to increase the likelihood of success. One year later, the company coasts to $10.6 million. Everyone gets bonuses and everyone is happy. But the problem is, everyone conveniently forgot they could have reached $11 million. The company set this mediocre plan, and that led to mediocre effort. They coasted into the harbor and reached the destination. So they succeeded. But did they really?"

"It doesn't sound like it," I reply.

"That's why it's important to set high-likelihood targets — but still *stretch*," Charlie says. "There's no room for mediocre efforts or mediocre results here. Too many leaders want their ship to feel like a cruise ship comfortably gliding around the Caribbean. You can tell most people on their team are coasting. They leave early from work. Accountability is low. Creativity is even lower. People are just satisfied with collecting their paycheck and clocking out. But what is the organization giving up when leaders accept that kind of mediocrity?"

"Probably a lot," I admit.

"Exactly," Charlie says. "Now, instead: wouldn't you rather run a high-performing crew boat from the America's Cup? One where everyone is working hard and sailing in the same direction? A win feels like a team win. You're exhausted — but you're victorious together, and the win feels that much sweeter."

"That does sound pretty awesome," I say. "It's like back in my high school football days. It was fun to win by four touchdowns against a smaller school who we knew we would beat. But it was way more satisfying to eke one out over the bigger rival school, who gave us more competition."

"Yep, you're on the right track," Charlie says. "Setting a stretch destination is all about reaching a destination that's a bit further or harder to get to than you'd anticipated. So for this example, let's say you set an internal target of $12 million. You start getting everyone off the vacation cruise ship, and onto the racing boat. You communicate to the team that $12 million is going to be a little bit of a stretch — but what's it going to take to get there? Here, let me show you."

Charlie gets out his own notebook and starts writing down numbers.

"At the $12 million target, you create a different vision and incentive structure," he says. "You'll pay your team twice their normal incentives of 200K if they meet it. If they reach $11.6 million, you'll pay 1.5 times their normal incentives. And at $10.6 million, they'll be paid 50 percent of their normal incentive."

I look down at the paper to see Charlie's roughly sketched-out chart of the bonus structure:

(MILLIONS)	STANDARD	PLAN A	PLAN B	PLAN C
REVENUE	10.6	10.6	11.6	12.0
BONUS	0.2	0.1	0.3	0.4
EBITDA	0.6	0.7	1.0	1.1
PROFIT INCREASE		0.1	0.35	0.5
PROFIT INCREASE %		16.7%	58.3%	83.3%

"This is a win-win scenario," Charlie explains. "By reaching for a further destination, your team was able to ship $1 million more in product than the previous year and achieve $1 million in pre-tax profit. We paid $100K more in bonuses than the standard. The company has $400K more in profit. And meanwhile, the team learned that by pushing themselves to reach further, they'll get rewarded, even if they don't fully reach their stretch destination."

My eyebrows raise at this possibility. Too many leaders I've worked alongside in the past have thought of goal-setting in the black and white: *Did we reach the goal or not?* But in looking down at Charlie's hastily scribbled notes, I see there was a totally different way.

How much further could Stackflow go using that structure?

"Now, three-year destinations," Charlie says. The man moves fast — I'm still just grasping the one-year concept.

"The three-year destinations are *on the way* to your longer-term vision," he continues. "They're the critical harbors you need to stop at before reaching your vision. They're the ones where you have about a 70 percent chance of success, so they're already stretch goals."

I start scribbling some numbers down on the paper between us:

In 2022, we finished as a $13.2 million company with $0.9 million in EBITDA (Earnings Before Interest, Taxes, Depreciation, and Amortization). The estimated current enterprise value — using a 4X multiple for small companies — is $3.6 million. Subtract $1 million in debt — for a net value of $2.6 million. (We paid $3.5 million for the company at the end of 2016!)

In three years, I want and need to sell the company to another ownership group to create liquidity for my original shareholders. But first, I need to pay out my existing shareholders with a good return. Their patience is already wearing thin. In this transaction, my personal harbor destination is to put aside the funds for college education and replenish retirement funds. I would like to continue with the new ownership group to take the organization to the next level (and a bigger payout). My vision is to have a new management team in place, then sell the rest of my shares or stay on as a board member.

So my goal — let's call it my destination — is $5 million in personal value (pre-tax) within three years. We need at least $10 million in value to reach this because I own 51 percent of the company.

I look up from my notes.

"To clarify, I don't want to be the only person who benefits from these deals," I say. "I want to make sure everyone who's committed to helping the company reach our destinations can benefit. My team really matters to me. They've put in their blood, sweat, and tears, and I want to make sure they earn part of the prize too. It would be amazing if our employees could earn enough money for a down payment for a house, or to help pay for college for their kids, or buy their dream car. That would give *me* fulfillment."

"I commend you for that," Charlie says. "When employees can share in a company's success, they tend to have way higher engagement. And it doesn't always have to be straight common stock. It could be long-term incentive plans, phantom stock, ESOPs, incentive stock options. It doesn't really matter. What's most important is there's a sense of ownership. That way, you'll know they're making decisions for the good of the company and to maximize value, even if it doesn't benefit them in the short run."

"Now," Charlie continues, reaching for his pen. "Let's get back to the value of your company. Without increasing that value in the short term, you're not going to be able to provide long-term monetary value to your employees. Let me repeat that: you won't be able to give long-term rewards to your employees without increasing the value of your company in the short term."

I pause for a minute. This delicate balance between short- and long-term decision-making had reared its head before. How often have I made short-term decisions to keep someone happy? Even if it wasn't in the best long-term interest of the company?

Hundreds, if not thousands, of times — over the past few years especially. It's felt like every decision has been about the short term: the pandemic, employee shortages, inflation challenges.

I once heard someone say, "Sometimes we must focus on the short run, because in the long run, we're all dead."

But in reality, Stackflow is going to die in the short run if we're not able to pivot.

That's what we did these past few years. And we overcame it. But we've become so short-sighted with our decision-making that we haven't set ourselves up to succeed down the road.

"Back to the numbers," Charlie says, pulling me away from my internal ruminations. "I know the numbers thing isn't necessarily your strength. You've always been focused on leadership and growth. Which has its own upsides. But growth for growth's sake doesn't always create more value."

Here, he pauses to write some notes for the 3-year destination:

Destination: $5 million in pre-tax personal value

Ownership: 51%

Company Target Value: $10 million (net of debt)

Anticipated Small Company Multiple: 4X

Company Target EBITDA: $10 million / 4X = $2.5 million

"To summarize," he says, "you would like to have $5 million in value from Stackflow within three years. You have 51 percent ownership, so the company would have to be valued at just over $10 million. If we assume the standard multiple for small companies at 4X, we need to have at least $2.5 million in EBITDA by the end of year three.

"So," Charlie continues, "what revenue will it take to earn $2.5 million EBITDA with the way things are trending?"

He starts sketching out charts on the paper in front of us:

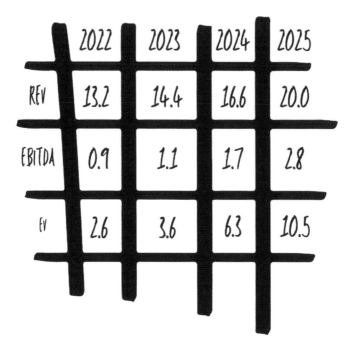

	2022	2023	2024	2025
REV	13.2	14.4	16.6	20.0
EBITDA	0.9	1.1	1.7	2.8
EV	2.6	3.6	6.3	10.5

By the time he's done, I'm exhausted just looking at all the numbers. I jump up to grab another refill of my coffee — I'm going to need it.

Chapter 12

The Right Numbers

"So, what do you see?" Charlie asks, pointing down at the charts between us. "What surprises you?"

At first, the wall of numbers just looks overwhelming. Growing from $13.2 million to $20 million in revenue seems like a massive jump. It seems like *everything* will need to change in order to make that happen: our sales approach, product flow, suppliers, customer service. All of it will need to shift.

But when I look at it from the perspective of year-over-year percentage growth, it's 55 percent over three years — about an 18 percent average each year.

Way more reasonable, I think, as I breathe a mini-sigh of relief.

The second thing I notice is that we'll have to grow even more than I originally anticipated because of the impact of inflation on the profits of the business. *Not* growing is not only going to decrease our net income — but it's going to make the company unsustainable.

I start to do some more of the math: we'll have to grow to $20 million, factoring in inflation. That will get us to $2.8 million in EBITDA. Multiply this by 4X and that's equal to $11 million. Subtract the estimated half-million in debt, and the net value would be $10.5 million. $10.5M x 51% = $5.4 million, which would exceed my $5 million destination.

A new sense of urgency bubbles up inside me. But this time it feels less like panic — and more like quiet confidence. I finally feel like I know the financial mechanics that will make this all work. I've been so lost in the fog of just surviving that I never stopped to really nail down the target we need to reach.

I close my eyes for just a second to take it all in. I feel a little hope again.

Charlie smiles. "Well, good news," he says. "We now have a reasonable level of confidence about what numbers we need to reach. Now, we have to figure out the *strategic* destinations that will get us to our *financial* destination. Keep in mind that valuation and all the numbers are the end result. But we only arrive at that result by focusing on shorter term, strategic destinations. And those destinations are going to require that you and everyone at Stackflow change some habits."

I feel excited about digging in.

"Most strategic plans focus on the end result," Charlie says. "For you, this means growing to $20 million in sales in three years, with a 50 percent gross product margin, and keeping operating expenses below $5 million, all to achieve a $2.8 million EBITDA. But here's the problem: these are all lagging indicators. They're not actually what we should be measuring and using to establish your short-term destinations."

I frown a little at this. *My* value was based on the bottom line, after all — not on strategic goals. I paid the team based on sales and income targets, not on operational initiatives. And our controller was either the hero or the scapegoat every period, based on whether we hit our financial targets. Those numbers are the ones we use to determine whether people get paid their bonuses or commissions. So why shouldn't they be guiding this strategic process?

I mention all this to Charlie, who nods in understanding — like he's heard this a million times before.

"Let me ask you a question," he says. "When your controller calculates your bonus, when does this take place?"

"After a quarter finishes," I reply.

"Did the controller have any impact on whether you *earned* the bonus? Or does he just calculate it after everything is said and done?"

"What do you mean?"

"Did the numbers change based on anything the controller did or didn't do?"

"Well, no," I say. "He just reports the facts."

"Exactly," Charlie says with a smile. "It already happened. The controller doesn't change the outcome."

I pause at this realization. He's right.

"Most strategic plans measure progress based on lagging indicators — things that have already happened, like sales numbers or net profit," Charlie explains. "Does the accountant who's calculating all that actually create more sales? Ship more product?"

"Definitely not," I say, thinking about our financial team — great at numbers, probably wouldn't be so great at sales.

"Exactly. So why are we focusing on the numbers that can only be calculated after a quarter is already over? You can no longer change the results. Unless you fudge the numbers, I guess — but that will get you fired. We should measure progress based on what's happening *along the way*. We need to focus on the *leading* indicators. You'll of course still calculate your accounting figures — sales and profit and all that. But those are all based on your leading efforts, which you should be keeping track of too. You need to focus your strategic efforts around what you can control, not what an accountant tells you after the fact."

This makes total sense, now that I take ten seconds to stop and process it. It's certainly logical. It's just *not* how I've operated or managed before.

I always ask my team, "Did you get the sale?" "Did you ship the product?" "Did you collect the payment?"

But these are all end results. I've been spending so much time rewarding or yelling at someone *after* they've already crossed the finish line — when in reality, I should be paying more attention to how they're running the race.

At the same time, as I was realizing just how logical this all was, I feel a wave of frustration too. *How could I have spent so much of my career on the wrong numbers?*

Charlie can sense my irritation.

"It's okay, Jack," he says. "You're not alone, trust me."

"So what now?" I ask.

"You need to figure out the key destinations your company needs to reach — on the way to the end result — that can be measured using leading indicators. This is what you're going to collaborate with your team on at the strategic retreat. This is where the bulk of your work together needs to be."

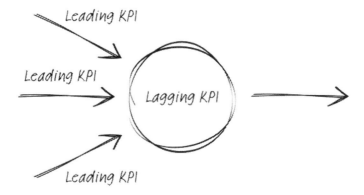

Finally, I'm starting to see a retreat agenda come into formation. No more of the endless brainstorming sessions, with no actual plan behind the ideas. This time around, I can already see a strategy taking shape — and an accountability structure to make sure we're actually executing on it. *Talk about what we've been missing all along*, I think.

As Charlie finishes his last dregs of coffee, I make a note in my calendar to finish up the strategic retreat agenda and email it to him the next day. He has another flight in the afternoon and will have time to review it.

I pack up my notes and head to my car with a renewed sense of purpose. The energy in the air feels practically palpable — and I can't wait to get home and tell Monica about all the progress we're making. Because this isn't just a win for me, or Stackflow. It's a win for her, too.

If only she saw it that way too…

Chapter 13

Connecting

As I walk in the front door, I can already feel all that energy I felt with Charlie loosening, like the air being let out of a balloon. Monica and I had another argument last night — and the atmosphere still feels charged when I get home. Clearly, it's still lingering.

I'm hardly the first CEO in the history of the world to argue with their spouse about working too many hours, or not being home enough, or slacking on the day-to-day stuff like laundry or taking care of the kids. Still, I never expected to be that CEO. My family means the world to me — and I feel a sense of failure every time I come home late or miss yet another family event.

Monica has always picked up the slack for me. And that's exactly what she's doing now: masterfully switching back and forth among preparing dinner, reviewing Daniel's homework, and cleaning the dishes.

I know I need to get back in her good graces, and she gets (rightfully) frustrated any time I ask her how I can help. Better to just jump in and do something, instead of wondering about it.

"Here, I'll work with Daniel on his homework while you finish dinner," I say. "We can tackle the dishes together later."

Daniel looks up from the kitchen table in surprise — and maybe a touch of suspicion. The last time I tried to help him with his homework last semester, we just got into an argument. I can't blame him for remembering that and feeling a little skeptical.

"What are you working on?" I ask, dropping into the chair beside him. I can see the open book in front of him before he even answers: pre-Calculus.

"We have a test coming up that I have to get an A on," Daniel tells me. "I won't get an A for the semester unless I get an A on this test, and that'll drop my GPA."

Daniel is 16, smart, and driven. He's already telling us about the colleges he wants to go to — top-tier schools that his mom and I would be thrilled to see him attend. But the standards at schools like that were sky-high. And so was the pressure. I know Daniel is stressed about keeping his perfect GPA, and I feel a snag of guilt about not being there for him more.

But now, with the conversation with Charlie still fresh in my mind, I actually feel like I have something in mind to help him.

"So, how is the teacher measuring this exam?" I ask. "How do you get an A?"

"Well, it's a 50-point multiple choice test," Daniel says. "I could get a 45 out of 50, and it would be enough for an A. Or I could even get a little lower than that, because there's an extra-credit assignment that could get me three more points."

"So, you could get as low as a 42 on the multiple choice, plus the extra credit question, and still get an A," I repeat back. "What have you done so far to prepare?"

"It's so frustrating," Daniel says, dropping his forehead into his hands. "I've taken three different practice exams, and I got a 37, a 38, and then a 40."

I reflect on my own experiences in any calculus-related class: those were pretty good scores. I'm impressed with Daniel's determination and effort. And based on those trends, he's improving — just not fast enough.

"Have you looked at what you've been missing?" I ask.

I get back an eye roll: classic teenage speak for "you're annoying, Dad." Still, he admits he hasn't focused much time on the questions he was missing.

"Let's go back and look at those problems and see if we can see any patterns," I say.

Sure enough, half the errors were related to factored polynomials. He'd made the other mistakes because he was working too fast.

"So it looks like we have two strategies to bump that test score up," I say, taking a pen and commandeering his pre-cal notebook:

#1: Review the polynomial formulas

#2: Slow down and double-check answers

I get another half eye-roll — "you don't have to write in my notebooks, Dad" — but I can see the same dawn of realization come over his face as I'd just had in that booth with Charlie.

Daniel jumps on YouTube to find a better way to understand the polynomial formulas (he's not going to get *that* explanation from me, after all).

A few minutes later, dinner is ready, and we set aside talk about formulas to instead discuss the game last night, and some of the drama happening at school. Monica's face has lightened up a bit from the frustration she showed earlier.

As I roll up my sleeves and start on the dishes after dinner, Monica takes the next half-hour to explain why she's been so upset. Daniel's at a critical time in school, and he could use both of our support. Plus, she's overwhelmed with taking care of everything at home herself. She knows how important work is — but she could use a little support here, too.

In the past, I've gotten defensive any time she brings up these frustrations. *I work this hard so we can afford the house, cars, and everything else we need.*

But I can see where she's coming from. I *have* been absent lately. And as I flash back to that CEO section of the vision I wrote, I know this isn't how *I* want to work either. For as much as I want to align my whole team around a vision for work, I know it's just as important to align with Monica on a shared vision for my role.

"I got it!" Daniel races into the living room and interrupts. "There's this genius on YouTube who explains those formulas way better than the textbook. I've been practicing those problems, and I'm getting a nine out of ten now. I think I'm finally ready now. Thanks, Dad!"

"Wow, awesome," I say, high-fiving him from the couch. "You've got this."

As I bring my hand down from the high-five, I glance at my watch. *Dang,* I think. *I still need to finish up the retreat agenda, so I can get it to Charlie in time.* I can feel the stress start pumping through my blood, and my body tenses up, knowing I still have a pile of work to finish before I can relax and go to sleep. Par for the course these days.

Monica can sense my almost-immediate change in demeanor. "What's wrong?" she asks.

I lean back against the couch cushions and thread my hands behind my head. Monica and I seem to be back on the same page after our talk — plus it would help if she understood some of the stress on my end too.

For the next hour, I open up to Monica about all the stress I'm feeling about the company: my uncertainty about whether it's going to return value, my sense of failure that it's not accomplishing everything I'd originally set out to do, my worry that we were going to lose our savings and retirements. It all just comes spilling out.

Still, I express the hope I felt a couple of hours earlier too: my meetings with Charlie, all the epiphanies I've already had because of what he's teaching me, and the confidence I'm starting to feel again about being able to bring Stackflow back as a winner. I tell her about the vision I've drafted, and all the excitement that's generated with the team.

"That all sounds amazing," she said. "It's been a huge worry for me, too — whether we're going to lose our retirement. But it sounds like you're getting closer to understanding the numbers. You know where you need to go and what you need to do. But *how* are you actually going to get there?"

It's hard to admit to her that, frankly, I don't know the answer to that yet.

Chapter 14

The SWOT Trap

5:05 a.m.: I jump straight out of bed.

Monica and I were up late talking through our frustrations, and I didn't have enough time to finish the retreat agenda. I know Charlie is waiting on it — and I have to get it to him before his flight this afternoon. So I throw on my clothes, grab my laptop, and head to the coffee shop, where I know I can put my head down and work uninterrupted for at least an hour or so before everyone starts needing something.

For the first 15 minutes, I don't type anything. I just think about what I actually want this retreat to be like. *Different from every other year,* I think to myself, with a touch of sarcasm. Of course, it needs to be different, because nothing ever gets done at the other ones.

This year's needs to be effective. But also inspirational. It needs to drum up the same level of excitement I feel when Charlie and I sit down for a strategy session.

I grab a pen and write notes on where we are:

What have we done so far?
- *Long-term vision*
- *SWOT analysis*

What have I done so far?
- *Financial projections*

What should we try to accomplish?
- *Identify our three-year destinations and our shorter one-year destinations.*
- *Draft potential "strategies" or how to arrive at the destinations.*

Agenda:
- *Review shared vision*
- *Input / review and adjust*
- *SWOT analysis*
- *Share financial projections (destinations)*
- *Input / review and adjust*
- *Determine strategic destinations that we'll need to reach in order to accomplish our three-year and one-year financial projections*
- *Set time to work with broader leadership on finalizing the strategies*

With a flourish, I send all my notes over to Charlie. He's probably already at the airport, which likely means he'll send over a reply in…

Yep, already a ping from him in my inbox. I've spent half an hour catching up on other work before heading to the office, and by the time I've cleared my inbox of everyone else's emails, Charlie's name pops right back up. That man is a machine.

He's added a line at the end to determine one-year strategic destinations, not just the three-year ones. Easy enough. And he also sends a note that he wants to talk more with me about how to make SWOT work for us.

Hmm. I'm not sure what he means by that. Seems pretty straightforward to me. Nevertheless, I reply and set up some more time for us to chat when he's back in town in a couple of days.

I think back to what I *do* already know about SWOT analysis. *Strengths, Weaknesses, Opportunities, Threats.*

Strengths and weaknesses are a measure of an organization's effectiveness. Finding the opportunities means evaluating how an organization could find new market success. And threats look at the *potential* risks in the future — whether they're environmental, or related to government restrictions, increased competition, inflation, or whatever else comes up.

Seems pretty simple to me, I shrug.

I know this model has been around for a *while*. According to Google, the Long-Range Planning Service at Stanford Research Institute created a report called *Formal Planning: The Staff Planner's Role at Start-Up* in 1965. That report included the four elements, and by the early 1970s, it had become the standard model for creating strategic plans. I'd basically never known anything different in my career.

But I start to frown a little as I start digging into some of the research. Maybe this approach isn't as cut-and-dry (or helpful) as I'd originally thought.

Two days later:

"You know, one of the most well-known strategists, Harvard professor Michael Porter, wrote *The Five Forces*, as a reaction to the SWOT model," Charlie explains, as we sit down for another lunch-hour coffee. "He thought SWOT analysis lacked rigor and was too ad hoc. And I have to agree. Managers overuse the SWOT as the 'internal facts' to understand where we are coming from and what challenges we have going forward… but there's rarely consistent follow-through on what comes out of it. Businesses — especially smaller businesses — do internal surveys for their SWOT analysis. But those are just people's opinions. You can see why I'm skeptical of an exercise that bases the entire future of an organization on untested assumptions and people's opinions about the truth. I'm more interested in the truth itself."

I see his point. After doing a little more research about the pitfalls of SWOT analysis, I see that maybe I've been steering my organization wrong this whole time. There could actually be a better way that I just never even thought to dig for.

"Plus, with SWOT analysis, there's often a disproportionate amount of time spent on things you can't even control, versus time spent on what you *can* control," Charlie says. "That focus on outside factors just leads you down the wrong path. For example, say you're selling medical equipment to schools. It doesn't matter that the medical industry is growing 20 percent per year. That doesn't mean *your sales* are going to automatically grow 20 percent per year, too. You need to think about what internal factors you have control over — not just notice what's happening externally."

"Frankly, I think SWOT analysis is a waste of time for most organizations," Charlie says. He's really on a roll now. "It really only works for huge organizations: think Fortune 500 companies who have the resources to conduct proper market research. They're usually hiring the McKinseys of the world to collect and validate their data. But here's the kicker: even the best consulting organizations in the world recognize that only about 10 percent of companies effectively use their data to effectively exploit market opportunities."

My eyebrows shoot up at that statistic. Really? Only one in ten companies are even properly using all that fancy data they're paying tens or hundreds of thousands of dollars for?

"The problem here is twofold," Charlie says. "You — and 99 percent of CEOs — are not in the Fortune 500. You can't (and shouldn't) afford McKinsey's rates. When I go into a company's strategic facilitation, they've usually already done a SWOT analysis because — well, it's what they know. They do it every year. So my job is to make their results more valuable, and make sure they're actually optimizing that data to create a better strategic plan."

"What do you usually notice?" I ask, curious to see if I've fallen into the same pitfalls as some of the others Charlie has worked with.

"Well, most organizations will treat each data point equally," he replies. "Then at the retreat, they'll go line by line and argue about each point. It's common to see nearly a full day wasted on things like 'possibility of Fortune

500 company taking away market share' or 'potential lawsuit seven states away.'"

I shift uncomfortably in my seat. I remember more than a couple of occasions at annual retreats where we've gotten carried away on a potential "threat" — and wasted precious hours talking about something that likely would never happen.

"So here's something I have them do instead," Charlie says, reaching for a piece of paper and his pen. "Have each person individually rank strengths by importance. For example, let's say you have 20 strengths listed for your team. Have every employee rank their top five strengths — but make sure they're making their lists *without* influence from their boss or any of their peers."

Charlie starts listing out some typical strengths on the page:

People
Teamwork
Excellent product
Location
Culture
Brand
Flexibility
Partnerships
Employee benefits
Founder support
Happy clients

"Now, after going through this exercise, you might see something like this," Charlie says, turning the page over and writing a new list. "The new list shows the top concepts based on a vote by the management team, with the total number of votes to the right. As noted below, five managers selected people as an important strength, four selected excellent products, and so on."

People: 5
Excellent products: 4
Happy clients: 4
Brand: 3
Partnerships: 2

"The value of prioritizing your strengths is that there's internal agreement," Charlie says. "Document and share this prioritization with everyone on the team to assure everybody agrees with the assessment and feels heard from the process. If someone objects to the list, let them air their thoughts, and then make adjustments as needed until you end up with a final strength's list."

"So what's the value of even having a strengths list in the first place?" I ask.

"Great question. We should be using our strengths to leverage growth. But on the other side… complete the same process with the company's weaknesses. The value of that list is that it'll give you a warning about which anchors are holding you back. You have to find a way to either remove or mitigate those anchors."

"But let's review this list again. People (5). So what does this really mean? Frankly, I rarely see a self-assessment that says that we have bad people. Our internal people are saying they think they are great, and they generally like most of the people that they hired. Did that really help us?

"Secondly, if we are going to use this information to support our strategic planning, we should gather more details. What is it about our people that is valuable? What are their engagement scores? How about employee turnover? For our products, what is our product margin, market share, and return rate? For clients, what is our customer concentration, market geography, and Net Promoter Score?"

"A handful of our larger clients, closer to $100 million (and a few of our smaller ones), will have the capabilities and resources to gather supporting metrics to validate the strengths, market share data, competitive positioning, etc.," Charlie continues. "This is the type of information Porter was looking for. Yet the majority of organizations use judgments to feed their plan because they don't have the expertise, knowledge, or time to analyze the information."

Oh, dear, I think to myself.

"What about opportunities and threats?" I ask, changing the subject. "Should we be doing some of these extra exercises around those sections too?"

"You got it," Charlie says. "Prioritize the specific opportunities, just like you did with strengths and weaknesses. But on top of that, list out each one in terms of potential dollar value, and how that relates back to your one- and three-year timeframes. Estimate the probability of each outcome occurring. So, say you have a 30 percent chance of closing a new $5 million deal. But you have an 80 percent chance of closing a new $3 million. Do the math for every potential opportunity out there, and you'll end up with a new, *weighted* list. That's going to help guide your strategic plan."

"I really like this idea," I say. "I can't tell you how many times we've circled around for hours, talking about the potential for an enormous, company-shifting deal — even though I know the likelihood of it happening is incredibly low."

"Exactly. This method reduces those kinds of discussions. Too many managers waste time at strategic retreats arguing about extraordinary opportunities with low probability of success. The sooner you can reduce that noise and lock onto doable ideas — versus feeling compelled to discuss a lottery winner for 45 minutes — the better."

"Now," Charlie continues. "Threats. Use the same prioritization process as before. Individual team members might feel really stressed about the next 'black swan' event — and those can happen. But spending too much time or energy worrying about it now isn't going to help. Assign those scenarios — and any other potential threat, even if it's smaller — probabilities and risk."

"But black swan events do happen," I say. "Just look at COVID…"

Charlie puts his hand up, seemingly already knowing what I'm going to say.

"If COVID taught us anything, it's that we should expect black swan events in the future, you're right," he says. "There has always been, and there will always be, black swan events. In recent history, think the Great Recession, 9/11, the dot.com bubble, etc. However, to 'predict' one of those events is usually a fool's errand. If a potential risk in your assessment is something like a fire, hurricane, earthquake, or virus, the best way to manage those challenges is to establish a solid risk management plan backed by insurance."

This strategy makes sense to me — and feels way more helpful than just throwing darts at the board and listing out every potential worst-case scenario with even a miniscule chance of happening.

"Regardless of your risk management plan, you need good insurance and three to six months of operating cash," Charlie says. "Those two pieces are critical if you want to keep your organization moving forward when the black swan event does take place. They'll give you the ability to make wise decisions, made from a place of security, versus not so smart decisions, made from a place of crisis. The difference in those two types of decision-making can be the difference between a company that flourishes and one that dies."

That last declaration settles into my gut. I already feel like Stackflow has been on the brink between those two outcomes — flourishing and dying.

We're not dead yet… but we certainly aren't thriving either.

Chapter 15

Building Harbors

How do I make the jump? I wonder, as Charlie flips a page in his notebook and starts scribbling again.

Stackflow is in this weird liminal space now between surviving and flourishing. But time is running out on pulling us back from the edge of that cliff.

"Now, what was the first thing I asked you to work on? What was the end result?" Charlie asks.

"The vision," I say, flipping to that page with all my notes. "And the destination is growing to a $10.5 million value by having at least $2.8 million in EBITDA in three years."

"And what would you expect to normally do next?" Charlie asks.

"We'd figure out the 'how' of getting there."

"Exactly. And your 'how' is going to be built using three pieces: your people, processes, and systems," Charlie says. "Think of yourself as the captain of the ship. You want to lead with clarity — and you've started this process well, by clarifying your vision. But this next step is critical. You want your team involved to get you to those critical harbor destinations on the way to that end vision. Think of these harbors as core infrastructure. Without them, you're not going to have the fuel or resources to reach your one-year or three-year destinations."

That last word bounces around my brain — and I realize I'm not quite getting the strategy terminology Charlie uses.

"Charlie, I'm a bit confused," I say. "I'm used to goals and strategies but can you help me understand why you'd say destinations instead?"

"Oh… Sorry, of course," he says. "I've been using this terminology for years, but sometimes take it for granted that people know what the heck I'm talking about."

"I call it the Strategy Hierarchy," Charlie continues, starting to sketch out a chart on the page in front of him. "At my firm, we always start with the top. This is your vision: the guiding lighthouse you are striving to reach in the long term. We recommend you have a vision that is ten years or longer into the future."

"Then," he says, drawing lines out from the "Vision" box, "we focus on what we need to reach within three years, in order to stay on target to reach the overarching ten-year vision. We call this three-year goal a 'destination.' That terminology injects more confidence that we're *actually* going to reach it."

He draws a few more lines.

"Then, we have one-year 'harbors,' or goals that will help us reach our 3-year destination. Think of these like the pit stop in the midst of a longer trip somewhere far away. You have to stop off at the harbors to refuel and keep making progress."

"That makes sense," I say, raising my eyebrows a bit. I'm not one for metaphors, but this one actually works.

"But we have to get even more granular. You know this as someone who's really detail-oriented. To reach our one-year harbors, we have to determine 'how' we're going to get there. We call these 'journeys' instead of strategies."

"Why is that?" I ask.

"Well, rarely do our strategies go in a straight line," Charlie says. "It's more of a hypothesis for how to reach our destination. But on a journey, we can move forward with our oars."

I chuckle a little.

"The oars?!" I ask.

"Yep," Charlie says. "The oars are the action steps (or tactics) to make our journeys (or strategies) work."

I look down at the rough chart Charlie's sketched out as he explains each step. And maybe it's because I know I've always wanted to buy a boat — who doesn't? — but this premise starts to click for me.

"So we have a vision," I repeat back. "And on the way to that vision, we have three-year destinations. To reach those, we need to stop off at our one-year harbors. We get there by mapping out a journey. And that journey is fueled by our oars — which are the actions to move our ship forward."

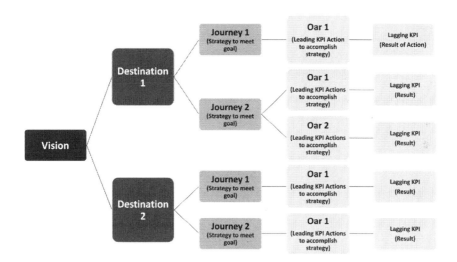

"So what are the kinds of questions I need to be asking during this retreat?" I ask. "How do we figure out what that infrastructure should look like?"

"Well, there usually needs to be change in all corners of your business when you are growing your business at double-digit rates," Charlie answers. "What are you going to need to change about your sales process in order to get where you want to go? Marketing? Your products and services? Operations? Customer service? Your employees? Partners and suppliers?"

"How do we know which pieces need to shift?" I ask. Changing that many pieces of the organization already feels overwhelming.

"When you're evaluating a process, think about whether it's creating new innovation," Charlie says. "Or you could ask this way: What's it going to take to double your speed to the harbor? And from a priority perspective, what is the most important harbor that you need to reach first?"

"Is that something I'm coming up with before the retreat, or is this a process everyone participates in?"

"Yes, the leadership team needs to participate," Charlie says. "They will be the ones to establish the harbors, so we can reach our final destinations. The best way to accomplish buy-in is having them help you determine the best way to get there."

"So, how do I get their buy-in?" I ask.

"Well, a pro-tip for facilitation is to allow individuals to write down their own ideas before sharing them with the group," Charlie says. "Then allow the participants to share what they've documented on a whiteboard or shared screen. This will help each person feel like they're part of the solution because they're seeing their work on the board. If you start by asking people individually, or worse, you start recommending what you want, they'll be swayed by that opinion. Remember, you pay their salary. Often the best ideas come from sources you don't expect. But eventually you'll take everyone's notes and consolidate them. Organize the ideas and combine the similar ones."

"Then — you guessed it — you want to rank each idea," he continues. "Use the priority weighting system we talked about with the SWOT process. Rank each idea according to its potential impact and the probability of it happening."

Already, this seems like way more of an organized process than I'm used to with these retreats. The whole process usually just ends in a giant tangle of ideas — some big, some small, some terrible, some great. But everything gets lumped onto the same whiteboard, and then none of them ever get a plan of action attached to them.

"Then you're going to want to take your top ideas and split your leadership teams into smaller groups," Charlie says. "Ideally, those groups are cross-functional. Give the groups enough time to figure out what critical functions they'll need in order to reach the harbor. Have each team present their ideas verbally to the whole group."

"Now, I highly recommend you take this next step," he continues. "The team members need to describe *why* the harbor is important. Verbalizing all this allows your team to actively listen and ask questions. It's incredible how this works in practice: A team will say things aloud, and every employee's confidence in the mission — and their place within it — either grows or wanes."

I do what Charlie has suggested and think of myself as the captain of a ship. And I know I only want crew members who are confident in where we're headed — not ones who will drop an anchor and keep us from moving forward. This part of the process feels especially important.

"You'll also want to clarify each harbor in one clear statement. For example, you've established that the first harbor needs to be building your sales team. Now — *why?* The more specific version of that statement is, 'We need to build our sales team to meet our incremental sales goals.' Okay, but you can get even more specific. 'We need to build our sales team to generate $4 million in incremental annual revenue in the next three years.'"

"But shouldn't there be something in the statement about *how* we're actually going to accomplish that?" I ask. My operations-heavy brain just wants to draw up a plan, yesterday.

"That's the hard part," Charlie says. "You don't want to dive further into developing the 'how' of hiring that sales team. That's later in the process — and you're going to want to include your team in building out the 'how' because that's how you drive buy-in."

"That makes sense…" I say, still itching to add strategic details to this statement Charlie is drawing up in his notebook.

"There are two problems with you adding in the 'how' at this stage," Charlie says, sensing my hesitation. "Number one is arrogance. You don't want to assume you know the best way to solve the problem. Most times, you don't. And number two is lack of ownership. You want your team members to *own* their harbors and how they are going to get there. You want them to believe it's their responsibility to reach them. If they have no say over how things get done, that's a lot less likely to happen."

"Now, back to this harbor statement," Charlie says, gesturing back down to the page. I thought we'd already gotten it down, but apparently not.

"We need to be even more specific," he says. "We need to add Key Performance Indicators — ways to measure how much progress we're making. For example, 'We need to hire three additional salespeople in one year to generate incremental sales growth of $4 million in the next three years.'"

I nod my head, finally understanding the level of detail these "harbors" were going to need if we were going to be successful.

And I finally feel like I have a handle on what we actually need to *do* at this annual retreat. In so many past years, the event has been all about *talking*. Hours-long conversations that don't end up going anywhere, brainstorming ideas that have a tiny probability of success, and then eventually leaving the weekend excited about all the potential goals — but with no strategy in place to accomplish them.

This finally feels different.

"Jack, you're ready," Charlie says. *How does he always seem to read my mind like that?*

"You've worked on your vision. You have a clear picture of where you want to be one and three years from now. You have a way to communicate that to the team. You have tools and processes ready to turn that vision into something action-oriented. You know how to design the strategy that will get you there. And you know to head into this weekend as an active listener — clear space for your team to talk and share ideas. Really listen to what they have to say. Be engaged. Don't assume you have the answers going in."

I take a deep breath, letting all of Charlie's advice sink in.

After months dreading this year's strategic retreat, all of a sudden, Thursday can't get here soon enough.

Chapter 16

Arriving at the Retreat

I'm more excited to kick off this retreat than I've been in years. And not just because of the surf and turf dinner I plan on ordering at Dooger's Restaurant, where I'm meeting the other five members of the leadership team to kick things off.

I feel ready to dive right into the agenda right at dinner — but I hold back and stick to the plan. As we sit down on the outdoor deck, I just say a quick thank you for everyone being there.

"Be ready for a momentous day starting at 8 a.m. tomorrow," I say.

Eyebrows rise all around the table. In attendance are Operations Manager Mike Roth, Marketing Manager Nancy Kline, Sales Manager Sandy Becks, Manufacturing Supervisor Dan Johnson, Controller Mark Holmes. In nearly every prior retreat over the past several years, we would kick the weekend off with a dinner like this one — eating and drinking way too much, then mutually agreeing to push the start time for the retreat itself back to 10 a.m. But not this year. Everything about this year feels different.

Still, all of that starts tomorrow. For now, we can just enjoy each other's company, the excellent food — and a little time away from significant others. This time around, I want to keep things focused around the company, so only team members have been invited.

One tradition does seem to continue this year: the conversation eventually shifting to the rivalry football game from the previous weekend.

The retreat is usually scheduled around the same time that the two rival universities play each other. It never fails to be a hotly debated topic. Two of the leadership team members went to the first school — a perennial contender — and another two went to the other school — the perennial underdog. The underdogs got to (finally) enjoy this night a little more than the blue bloods. Mike from operations, especially. He's a huge fan, and usually spends more than a few minutes at these annual dinners getting ribbed when his school's been run over by three touchdowns.

"How many times did they go for it on fourth down and fail?!" Mike asks as he grabs another beer. It's a rhetorical question: We all know it was five times. "And the head coach just didn't take responsibility. Sometimes those coaches forget who pays their salary. But he's young — maybe he'll learn from this."

We all nod in agreement, moving onto the next piece of the conversation — which Mike decides needs to be about supplier delays.

I know Mike's having some problems at home because of how many hours he's working. So with the new complaints, it seems like he's letting off a little steam.

After one dessert shared amongst everyone at the table, the waiter brings the check.

"I'm excited to see everyone tomorrow morning at eight," I say as I sign the receipt and add a generous tip. "There will be a continental breakfast in the conference room, and we'll kick off the agenda then."

We all walk back over to the hotel where we're staying next door.

"Hey, Jack. Want to do a nightcap here at the bar?" Mike asks, gesturing to the bustling hotel bar to the right of the front doors.

"No, thanks," I say. "I want to review all the materials one more time before we kick off tomorrow morning. But you all go ahead."

Sandy and Mark take Mike up on the invite, while Dan and Nancy look relieved to follow my lead and use the excuse to not join.

The elevator dings on our floor and I say goodbye to the rest of the team as I head back to my room. Everything about this year does feel different — including the little bundle of nerves *(or is it excitement?)* I feel about finally kicking this retreat off.

Chapter 17

Retreat Kick-off

5:07 a.m.: Enough lead-up. It's go time. I wake up to two text messages — one from Monica and one from Charlie.

"Good luck, Jack — you got this!" reads the one from my wife. I responded with a "Thank you, I needed that" and a heart emoji.

Charlie has texted, *"This is a new beginning. Remember: listen to learn. Be the captain that inspires your team and steer the ship where it needs to go."*

It's at this moment that my muscles tense up and my heart starts racing a bit more than normal.

Can I really be that leader?

I go back to my notes and presentation deck, making a couple minor changes. But for the most part, I'm as ready as I'll ever be. Now is just the time to act.

7:35 a.m.: I arrive downstairs at the hotel conference room, and Sandy is already there. I'm a little surprised because she went out late last night. But she's always a professional, and you would have never known by her appearance. The rest trickle in as the hotel waiters serve breakfast.

We start chatting about everyone's holiday plans, waiting on the last arrival. Mike rushes into the room at 8:23 a.m. — pretty uncharacteristic of him to be late for something. Then again, we do usually push the start time to 10 a.m. to make room for late-night beverages. I can tell that Mike wishes we'd done that this year — he barely nibbles his toast while everyone else piles their plates high with bacon, eggs, and pancakes.

As we wrap up breakfast, I connect my laptop to the room's big-screen, and navigate to my first PowerPoint presentation. I start passing out a fresh notebook and three sticky-note pads to each person. Some eyebrows raise around the room — this already feels more participatory than our past retreats.

The hotel staff has left a whiteboard and several markers at the front of the room, too, and I grab a black one to start writing. Instead, I kick things off with a mini-speech.

"Team, I haven't been this excited about Stackflow since I first took over the business five years ago," I say. "But I'm also concerned that if we don't make changes, we're not going to get where we want to go. We're not going to reach the vision."

I notice a couple in the room shift uncomfortably in their seats. Change is never easy, especially when we have a veteran leadership team who can be a bit set in their ways.

"Our vision is our driving force," I continue. "To reach the future we want, we need to double in size in order to meet our profitability targets. We should have reached those targets two years ago — but you all are well familiar with the challenges we've had since 2020. COVID. Labor shortages. Increasing wages beyond what any of us would have expected. Inflation that none of us has seen since the '70s and '80s. The cost for everything has hit record highs: transportation, commodities, materials. And just when we thought we'd had enough, the Fed decided to kick a dog while it was down, and raise interest rates to levels we haven't seen since the 1980s.

"With your extraordinary efforts over the past couple years, we've grown our revenues to record highs. I really appreciate everyone's tireless effort. It doesn't go unnoticed, and we couldn't have done any of this without you."

I pause, then start clapping. At first, everyone's a little confused and doesn't know what to do, but they eventually join in too. Sandy even cheers a little, inspiring everyone to raise their hands up in the air and finally celebrate. After all the chaos of the past couple years, we haven't spent any time actually celebrating. Every moment was just about surviving another day.

And we *had* survived. Other companies certainly had not.

I let that little burst of joy sink in. Then I go over to the whiteboard and write:

2019 sales: $10M

2022 sales: $13.2M

32% growth — congratulations!!

"There is a 'but' to all this," I say.

It's time to get grounded.

"To reach that goal, it came at a huge cost. Because of all the price increases across the board, our profits are lower than they were prior to buying the company. To make money in the future, we're going to have to earn it the old-fashioned way: by *earning* it." Several of the younger leaders did not remember, nor appreciate, the classic commercial from E.F. Hutton.

Now I have everyone's attention — even if they're a little confused.

"Later today, I'm going to show you the numbers," I continue. "But before that, let's start out from a position of trust. I'll let you know straight-up where we need to be: This is the goal we need to spend the next couple of days designing a strategy to reach. We need to become a $20 million company in the next three years."

I let the gravity of my words wash over the room.

"This is *not* just a nice-to-have," I say. "To become a viable long-term company, we need to reach $20 million to keep our bottom lines sufficient. To get there, we're going to have to change our way of doing things. And I'm not talking about incremental change. I mean *substantial* change. We're going to need everyone on board the ship. And we need to remove all the anchors that are holding us back."

More uncomfortable seat-shifting.

"But we don't just want to move to get to a number," I say. "We want to move with a purpose. This three-year destination — to become a $20 million company — is critical to return to profitability and to pay back our original investors."

I look around the room, and I'm met with a mix of emotions. Some are sitting forward in their chairs, listening intently. A couple seem to be avoiding eye contact. There's palpable excitement — and fear.

Are they mirroring *my* emotions?

"Today, we're going to focus on possibilities," I say. "We're going to review the ten-year vision to make sure we have a clear compass to the future. Then we'll review what we need to accomplish in order to make our three-year destination a reality. And then we'll hone in on the journeys that will get us there."

"Tomorrow, we'll shift gears. Tomorrow is about focus. So allow yourself to think and dream freely today. We'll have enough time tomorrow to focus on the strategy behind the ideas."

I turn back around to the whiteboard, then pause with the marker in my hand. Charlie's voice pops in my head: "Listen to learn, Jack. Get your team's input and buy-in to this destination."

I spin back around, and gesture to everyone's notebooks and sticky notes in front of them.

"Now," I say. "Let's get started."

Chapter 18

The Plank

Two hours later, notes cover the room. There are scribbles on the whiteboard. Sticky notes litter the conference table. Notebook pages are strewn about with half-formed ideas sketched out.

A plan is coming together. And I can actually feel the energy in the room start to shift. Some of that fear I sensed earlier might just be transforming into excitement.

"Okay, folks," I say. "Let's take a quick break and come back to this in 15."

A few people take a restroom break and return to the room; everyone is chatting in their own separate conversations. The only person I see standing alone is Mike. I migrate over to his side of the room, and try to make small talk about the upcoming football games this weekend. But he's having a hard time looking me in the eye. Sensing something is up, I ask if he wants to take a quick walk somewhere else.

We stroll back out the front door of the hotel to get some fresh air. I want desperately to fill in the gap — to figure out whatever it is missing — but I hold off.

Finally, Mike turns toward me, and I can tell he has something to say.

"Jack, I'm really concerned," he says. "You know, I work like crazy to keep the operations running. I'm here every day of the week. And this has put a real strain on my marriage. Karen might leave me."

He swallows hard, trying to keep his emotions in check.

"On the surface, this whole company vision seems really exciting," Mike continues. "I've always wanted to be part of a company that doubles in size. That's why I've put in the amount of work that I have. And as you know, the challenges the past few years have been incredibly difficult. We had to deal with the COVID protocols. We had a tough time bringing people back to the office. We had to raise wages. But I still lost some really great people through that process. And you already know hiring was a nightmare. How many people ghosted us and never showed up even after accepting an offer? I still don't understand how people thought that was okay."

I nod my head, rolling my eyes.

"At least three people," I say, remembering how frustrated everyone was — especially Mike.

"Then after we finally thought we were getting a handle on labor, the material shortages compounded everything," Mike says. "There were freight shortages, and all the shipping times got extended, even though our shipments were already late. The customers seemed to understand, but patience really grew thin after a while. And no matter how many times we asked our vendors for better results, they just said, 'Oh, it's freight,' or 'It's labor shortages.' Name your excuse. No one took responsibility for anything."

Sandy pops around the corner to check on us. I wave her away with the "five more minutes" gesture. I'm starting to think it might take double that: Mike is really on a roll, and I don't think we've gotten to the heart of what's actually on his mind.

"Then the material costs just kept climbing," he continues, not seeming to even notice Sandy coming and going. "We had to spend triple the time hunting for deals that just didn't exist. Our suppliers would say, 'This is our quote for today only.' It's just been so difficult, and I feel like I've let you down. Our customer delivery times are on time only about 30 percent of the time, our lead time has doubled, and our product margins are down."

I don't say anything. I know how challenging the past couple years have been — and I don't doubt Mike's work ethic. I see the number of hours he puts in every week, and the number of times I walk by his office at 7 or 8 p.m. and he's still there.

"I recognize that this next year has the possibility to be different," Mike says. "But how different? There are still labor challenges. Commodity costs have come down some, but they're still nowhere close to the old rates. And now these interest rates have put a new pressure on our line of credit. So as we look to increase sales as much as you say we need to… I don't know how I can do it. There's only one of me, and I feel like I've been failing for the past three years."

Mike looks down at the ground.

So, there it is. How many of my other team members feel this way too?

"Mike, we've never worked in an era like this," I say. "The Great Recession was definitely difficult, but this has been different. I appreciate all the arduous work you've put in. I really do. And if you need to take some time off to be with your family, I completely understand."

Mike looks back up at me and shakes his head. My stomach drops a little at the look on his face.

"I'm going to leave the company, Jack," he says. "I've been interviewing with different companies, and I already have one offer in hand."

"Mike, if we need to talk about a salary bump —" I start to say.

But he cuts me off. "I'm not doing this to raise my salary," Mike says. "I just need to find a different job — one with less responsibility, so I can spend more time at home."

I feel like I've been sucker punched in the gut. How can Mike just quit? Especially right now? After everything that we've gone through together?

He's been with the company since the beginning, and his institutional knowledge is only matched by his work ethic. I feel shell-shocked that he would walk away from the company, right when we need him the most.

Just as quickly, my focus shifts back inside to the whiteboard in the conference room. All those lofty numbers and goals…

How are we going to do this without Mike?

Chapter 19

Jumping Ship

Despite all the worries (and to-do lists) immediately hammering through my mind, I try to zoom back to the current moment. *We're right in the middle of a strategic retreat*, I think.

"Mike, thanks for sharing all this with me," I say. "I have to admit, I'm really surprised. But I do understand. This is important for you and your family, and I respect your decision. We're going to miss you. When do you plan to leave?"

"At the end of the decision-making process, I'll commit to giving you 30 days to help with the transition," Mike answers. "I'll always be available to you and the team for questions."

I let out a little sigh of relief. I really appreciate Mike being willing to stay on for those 30 days — and I know he'll hold up his end of the bargain. It's a nice gesture to offer to answer questions from the new personnel.

Now, the clock starts ticking. I need to find a replacement within about 45 days or less.

"If possible, can you keep this between us until you announce the 30-day transition?" I ask.

Mike agrees, which fills me with even more relief. There's no sense in getting everyone else worried (or gossiping) before we have a plan in place.

"Do you want to continue working with us on strategy here in person?" I ask. "Or would you rather head home?"

"Thanks for asking," Mike answers. "I'm actually really interested in continuing. Getting this off my chest will help me stay more engaged. And I genuinely care about the company's future. I want to provide whatever input I can to help create a plan that works."

"Thank you, Mike."

It always feels curious to thank someone… right after they punch you in the gut.

"Why don't you head back into the conference room, and I'll be there in a few minutes," I say. "I'm just going to run to the restroom."

I decide to walk to the one on the other side of the hotel lobby, just to give myself some time and space to think before heading back in to talk to the team — and pretend like everything is okay.

Wow. Mike is leaving.

I really need to talk to Charlie about this. But his voice pops into my internal thought pattern: "Remember, Jack, you're there to *listen* to your team."

So I pause — and replay my conversation with Mike, so I can really listen to what he had to say.

Mike told me he's leaving for two main reasons:

One, he's working too hard, and it's impacting his family life. And two, he couldn't see himself working harder to help the company grow to the next level.

Maybe this is actually a blessing in disguise.

Mike never lacked responsibility, nor effort. He could sometimes be a bit difficult to work with, because he was pretty set in his ways. But since he was always able to get things done, I normally left him alone. But to get the company to the next level, I know we're going to have to change. *I'm* going to have to change. Our processes are going to have to change. So maybe it's the best Mike is bowing out now. Maybe this will actually make my job six months down the road a lot easier. This can be an opportunity to get the *right* person in place to do the job.

I go over the past... how long has it been? I look down at my watch, and somehow it's only been 20 minutes since we started our break. In that span, I've gone from stunned to uncertain to... hopeful.

Just another day as a CEO, I chuckle to myself. Time to get my head in the game and get back to work.

Chapter 20

Journeys

Within a couple of hours, we're close to identifying all our key journeys to reach our three-year destination — the ones we believe will be necessary on the way to our $20 million goal.

On the whiteboard, I list out what everyone has come up with:

#1 Develop a growth-oriented sales team

#2 Identify a new market to sell our products

#3 Create new website to reflect our market position

#4 Increase manufacturing capabilities

#5 Implement new ERP system

#6 Improve customer service

#7 Become a wonderful place to work

I look at our list of seven. Initially, I'm pretty satisfied with them. I know the goal here is to brainstorm and get all the best ideas on the table. But looking at them again, I start to get a little concerned.

Are we really capable of achieving these and getting to the next level?

I ask the team to clarify each of the journeys. I write out a few questions I want everyone to think through before answering:

What is the outcome of each journey in three years?

What will we need to complete one year from now?

How will we measure success?

Will this increase our sales?

Will this improve our efficiency?

Will this improve our bottom line?

What is the likelihood of success?

I break the team into pairs, and they start brainstorming together.

Initially, everyone struggles with the first question. Everyone knows it's just an estimate. So how is it possible to really know the answers?

Within 45 minutes, they've mapped out the journeys to the destination:

We need $6.8 million in additional revenue to reach our $20 million, three-year destination. We'll need incremental sales of $4 million in Year 3. Our existing sales team will have to sell a total of $10 million, compared to the $8 million they provide today. That will give us a total of $14 million. The remaining $6 million would come from growing our existing accounts with our account management team, compared to the $5.2 million they provide today.

EXISTING SALES TEAM	8.0	8.5	9.0	10.0
NEW SALES TEAM	0.0	0.5	2.0	4.0
ACCOUNT MANAGEMENT	5.2	5.4	5.6	6.0
TOTAL SALES	13.2	14.4	16.6	20.0

In one year, we'll have to hire two of the three salespeople. We'll divide our sales team by four different industries. Sales members within the same industry will divide geographies.

I finish outlining their ideas on the whiteboard, then turn back to the team and ask the same question I'd written before:

"Will this increase our sales?"

Everyone around the room nods their heads.

"We think so," Sandy says. "From an efficiency perspective, we believe breaking everything down by industries will help our teams be more effective with sales opportunities."

"Plus, we have limited market share in the Southeast and Midwest. If we strategically place the new sales reps in those markets, we should be able to connect with accounts that have eluded us for years."

"Yeah," I say, nodding my head along and starting to get excited. "If we create $4.5 million of incremental sales, plus existing sales team members increase theirs by $3 million, and if we have a gross profit percentage of 50 percent… then this will generate $6.6 million in EBITDA prior to operational expenses."

"So," I continue, "what about the likelihood of success of this plan?"

"We estimate it as between 70 and 80 percent," Sandy answers. "Our teams will be more focused on construction and engineering firms that are growing, where we have existing sales."

At this moment, I feel like we're on the right track. It's a relief, especially as the news from Mike still feels fresh in my mind.

We keep going through the same questions for each of the journeys, until we come up with a whole chart.

	#1	#2	#3	#4	#5	#6	#7
3 YEAR JOURNEY	7.5M SALES	NEW VERTICAL MARKET	NEW WEBSITE	2ND SHIFT	NEW ERP	20% HIGHER REPEAT BUS	IMPROVE EMPLOYEE RENTENTION
SALES	7.5M	1.0M	INCREMENTAL	INCREASE CAPACITY BY $6M	UNKNOWN	2.0M	?
SUCCESS	75%	40%	25%	70%	70%	60%	50%
EBITDA NET	2.7M	0.2M	?	1.7M	NEGATIVE	0.6M	?

By the time we finish, I can already start to see what we should be trimming in order to focus on what's most important. But that's not on today's agenda.

In fact, nothing else was on today's agenda: It was already 5:48 p.m. We'd been working with so much concentration I didn't even realize it was time for dinner until one of the hotel employees knocked on the door to tell us the food would be ready at the top of the hour.

We pack up our materials and start migrating over to the dining room. There's a lot of energy throughout the team, and everyone is in a good mood. Even Mike has been participating fully, and no one else seems to have a clue he has one foot out the door already.

I feel really pleased with the final exercise. It felt clarifying to see all the journeys laid out like that.

I thought back to how helpful and optimistic everyone was throughout the process — well, except Mark. There had been a point where we were talking about the increased sales, and Mark, our controller, got a little defensive. He tried to explain that our current system wasn't going to be able to manage all the additional transactions. More importantly, the system was out-of-date and no longer even supported for upgrades. The software provider had moved to cloud-based solutions.

My immediate reaction was to start going down the rabbit hole of better tech solutions. But then I stopped — this was tactical, not strategic. If we're going to have to replace our accounting system anyway, why would this go in the strategic plan? This first day was supposed to just be about the *what* and *why:* We will worry about the *how* later.

At dinner, I maintain my one-drink limit again, the same as last night. It was nice this morning to wake up feeling fresh and not having to battle a hangover as we dove into numbers and strategic ideas.

I look around the table, and I'm surprised to see that the rest of the team has followed suit — even Mike.

Chapter 21

The Anchor

Focus.

That's the only word I write on the whiteboard the next morning. I underline it twice for emphasis. Today's agenda is all about focus: nailing down the biggest priorities that will have the most outsized impact and drive us toward our desired outcomes.

"Most organizations only complete about two-thirds of their strategic objectives," I explain. "This is because of a variety of problems. Why do you think that is?"

"Lack of vision," Sandy says. I write that on the board.

Mike adds, "No buy-in from the team."

"Good one, Mike," I say as I add it to the list.

"We're unclear where we're going," Dan says.

"The journey doesn't have an ROI," Mark says.

Well, that's ironic, I think.

"The chances of accomplishing the journey are a long shot," Sandy says.

"Or we're too busy!" Nancy adds.

I scribble all the ideas on the board and put an exclamation mark on Nancy's.

"Nancy, that is the number one reason strategic plans fail," I say. "You're unable to reach your new destination because you simply have too much on your plate. And that's a big, valid reason, too. But this year, we're going to do things differently. We're going to focus on only a few things that will have the biggest impact. Then we'll work on the next initiatives only after the first ones have been completed."

"And honestly, this will be really hard," I continue. "The biggest reason it's going to be difficult is… because of me. I'm the reason we typically fail. I ask everyone to do too much. I don't set aside the right number of resources for you to get things done. And I never really ask about the key initiatives: I only ask about sales, shipping logistics, and all those day-to-day things that bog all of us down.

"Going forward, I'm going to try to not be the obstacle keeping you from being successful. I need to let you all sail the boat — and stop being the anchor."

I see at least one jaw drop as I look at everyone's faces. I'm not sure anyone would have expected that I would admit to all that. Time seems to stand still as everyone processes what I just said.

Finally, Sandy speaks up.

"I've known you for five years and I don't recall you ever saying something like that before," she says. "I want to thank you. But at the same time, I have to admit — I don't fully trust it. Can we call you out in the future? How do we make sure you remember this conversation?"

"That's a fair question," I say. There have been times when I've even wondered the same thing myself. I've spent a lot of years being the bottleneck, so it's going to be tough to pull myself out of the habit — and become the visionary the team really needs.

"We should hang that anchor around your neck," Dan says.

Now everyone turns to look at him, puzzled.

"What do you mean?" I ask.

"No, really," he says. "We should get an anchor and put it on a big necklace. You know, like Mr. T used to wear. Or the 'turnover chain' you see in college football. Every time a player fumbles or throws an interception, they have to wear the turnover chain around the sidelines."

I crack up.

"That's actually hilarious," I say. "I hate those turnover chains! So having one of those would be a good wake-up call. Now, here's another question: Can I put the turnover chain on other team members if they're being an anchor?"

Everyone agrees: Equal-opportunity turnover chain-wearing seems like the fair thing to do.

Before I know it, Dan has pulled up his computer and is searching online for the materials we need to make our own version of the turnover chain — the anchor chain.

We even come up with a sign to post on the wall once we get back to the office: *Don't be the anchor.*

I love how involved everyone has gotten. And I love even more the idea of finally escaping the habit of holding everyone else back.

Chapter 22

The Right Journeys

Now that we've decided no one is going to hold us back, it's time to really answer the big question: *How are we going to move forward?*

I head back over to the whiteboard from yesterday, where we'd drawn up the table for our journeys.

"So, after reflecting on all this from yesterday, does anyone have anything to add?" I ask.

Mark raises his hand.

"I don't think we fairly evaluated the ERP system," he says.

"Okay, tell me more," I say.

Mark spends the next five minutes telling us how if we upgraded the system, sales orders could move more quickly and inventory would be easier to locate. Most importantly, he says, we need to make the change because the product will no longer be supported in 12 months.

These all seem like reasonable thoughts. But I remember the conversation I had with Charlie about narrowing in on what's *most* important — and what will drive the *most* impact.

"Will a new accounting system help us get more sales?" I ask.

I can tell that Mark wants to answer yes. But there's no clear data to assume that would be true.

"No," he admits.

"Will the new system decrease our operating expenses?" I ask.

"Well, I believe we'd be able to process transactions faster with a new system," Mark answers.

"But would it decrease operating expenses?"

Mark pauses and thinks for a minute.

"We have two people who process orders today," he says. "I believe with a new system, we'll only have to increase that group by one instead of two when we double in size."

"How do you know?" I ask.

"It's just an estimate."

"Okay, let's assume we don't have to hire the additional headcount until halfway through year two. How much would that save us?"

"About $25,000 in year two and $50,000 in year three."

"What will be the costs to buy the new system? The annual SaaS costs?"

"I anticipate it would cost us about $40,000 more per year."

"And what about the implementation costs?"

"That would likely be another $50,000."

"Okay, let's do the math," I say, grabbing a marker.

$75,000 in savings

$40,000 x 3 = $120,000 + $50,000 implementation for $170,000 in total costs.

The project would have a negative $95,000 impact on the bottom line.

Seeing the numbers up on the whiteboard, Mark looks a little dejected. He tries one more time.

"Based on this analysis, it doesn't seem to be a high-priority decision," he says. "This also doesn't measure the internal costs to implement the system. I'm sure there are more potential efficiencies. But I don't see how they'll beat out the other prioritized strategies."

Dan from manufacturing chimes in.

"I do agree we'll have to make a change to the system," he says. "But today, that's not our biggest bottleneck. The biggest risk I see is not being able to upgrade the system down the road. However, we haven't done an upgrade in three years, and it's still functional. Frankly, it's been nice not having to do an enhancement, because we tend to have a work stoppage while those occur. Those lost days of shipping can be really costly."

"I agree we'll need to make an accounting system upgrade eventually," I say. "Probably sooner than three years. But based on these ROI calculations, it seems like it may cost us more than it will create value, at least at this stage."

"If we see this growth that we're planning for, and we begin to see more challenges, can we readdress this issue?" Mark says.

"Absolutely," I say.

"Okay, then I'm on board with not including this in the current strategic plan," Mark says.

I thank Mark for bringing up his concerns and fighting for his position. Even if he initially disagreed with what we were planning, this is exactly the type of engagement I want to see in this process.

Sure, this took an additional 25 minutes that I hadn't included in the agenda. But to keep my controller focused and in alignment with our plans, it was well worth the extra time.

"Okay, so from an ROI perspective, here are the top three journeys," I say, raising my arm to start writing again.

1) *Expand sales team — net $2.7 million*
2) *Implement second shift to increase production capacity — net $1.7 million*
3) *Increase repeat business — net $0.6 million*

"Now, let's assign leadership roles for each of these areas," I say.

1) *Expanding sales team — Sandy, sales*
2) *Second shift — Dan, manufacturing*
3) *Increase repeat business — Sandy, sales*

I'm just about to move on to the next item on the agenda when Mike raises his hand.

"Jack, I thought we were going to focus more," he says.

I look up in surprise.

"What do you mean?" I ask. "We've narrowed everything down to three key destinations."

"No, I mean on the leadership side."

I look back at the whiteboard. He's completely right.

From an organization standpoint, we shouldn't have a leader focusing on more than one journey at one time — and Sandy has two.

"And let's look at this from a different perspective," Nancy says. "Repeat business is as much of a function of customer service as it is sales. Let me take on this role."

I look around the room. Everyone is nodding in agreement — even Sandy.

"When you think about it, Jack, I'm going to have interviews, training, and industry/territory relocation efforts to get everyone to agree to these changes," she says. "We also want there to be incremental sales. We don't just want to cannibalize existing sales channels. We will want to talk with our existing key customers to assure we are serving them well. Nancy is great at researching and understanding the customers' needs, and then we can apply these messages to our account management team and to future marketing campaigns. And I hadn't mentioned this earlier, but I may need to make one or two changes with my existing team."

I immediately know the team is right on this one. And I also know how this whole process would have gone in previous years: No one would have thought twice about someone taking on multiple responsibilities. Plus, we would have tried to grab all seven of the journey concepts — and probably a couple more. Each person would have had at least two or three or more on their own.

That tactic felt even crazier now, knowing how many hours everyone was already working. No wonder we never actually moved forward on our biggest strategic plan ideas. Everyone's heads were just down to the grindstone, working, working, and working — never looking back up to gauge the big picture.

At this point, I'm really grateful to the team for really buying into this process — and helping me see my blind spots.

"I totally agree," I say. "Congratulations, Nancy, you're the leader for the repeat business journey."

Everyone in the room starts applauding, and Nancy looks up with a big smile.

Chapter 23

Defining Our Actions

We had danced around this part of the process, but hadn't fully dived in yet. I know it's on everyone's mind. And I have to admit it's on mine too: Sure, these journeys are all great and exciting. *But how on earth are we actually going to get there?!*

I take a marker and draw a mini-diagram on the whiteboard:

Starting point → Journey "The How" → Oar "The Action" → Destination

"How we get from the starting point to our destination is a journey," I explain. "That journey is what's in the middle, from the beginning to the end. Rarely is it a straight line, though. Today, we're going to draft the 'oars' for each journey. Notice I said the word 'draft.' We're going to establish the actions that need to be taken to complete our shorter term journey and reach our long-term destination. We're going to stop ourselves from completing the full details of the oars: those are the details of what it's going to take. Think of the oars as the energy or power we're going to need to successfully complete the journeys."

"I also want to admit I've gone about these strategic retreats all wrong in the past," I continue. "We have a tendency to just hear ideas from the top-down. But in reality, it's the ones doing the work on a day-to-day basis who often have the right ideas. We always return from these strategic events on a 'high' about all the exciting ideas we came up with — and then we don't allow those who are going to do the work to have a say in the matter."

"Remember what's happened in past years?" I ask.

Mark speaks up: "I remember when I *didn't* attend these events. You, Mike, and Sandy would be all excited when you came back to the office. I would always feel a little jealous. And on top of that, I'd feel a little bitter after I saw the bills from the event. On the outside, it always felt like a big waste of time and money. Third, you'd always come back with so much confidence, and it felt really arrogant. We know you're the leaders, but for many of you, you weren't in the trenches doing the 'dirty work' for years. Sometimes that can lead to detachment from reality."

"Every product, every process, every system, every invoice, every person has details," Mark continues. "And often, you're completely unaware of them. So when you say, 'We're going to do this or that,' we know you don't… exactly know what you're talking about. Yes, you get the big picture, but you're not always aware of what it's actually going to take to get there."

Mark is really in a groove now. By the looks on everyone else's faces, you can tell there's some amazement that Mark has the courage to say what he's saying. But no one is jumping in to argue, and I see a couple of head nods. I can tell that no one in the room thinks he's wrong. So I keep listening.

Mark takes a breath and continues.

"So when this happens, we know we can't say much," he says. "We need to follow the orders. Even when a journey seems like the right idea, we get frustrated because we don't have a lot of say in the matter. Rarely does anyone speak up, because they know they'll seem insubordinate. Or if it's not insubordination, we'll be told that we're not being 'strategic' or we're not being a 'team player.' We're told that we don't get it."

"But the problem," he says, shifting forward in his seat, "is it's usually the leaders who don't get it. We're the ones doing the work. Sometimes there's even a quiet mutiny — that's when we'll just listen and nod our heads. We're not necessarily agreeing with what's going on; we're just acknowledging what's being said. The leader thinks we're on board. And then we do nothing except work. We simply tell our leader that we're busy — and we usually are.

There are customer complaints, vendor issues, and employee problems. Most leaders will recognize that we're too busy to really move forward with whatever big change or initiative they wanted to do, and the next thing you know, that strategic idea is gone.

"And then the next week, the leader will be discussing some great book they're reading, and, oh, we should try this strategy. They're always on to the next great idea. It feels like they're just kind of blindly walking the plank. They think they're doing a fantastic job and being considerate of the team. But in reality, they're just failing to make any change because they didn't have the patience for it to get done. And a lot of this could be solved if they just asked one simple question: How would *you* get this done?"

I nod my head in understanding. I can't blame him for being more concerned about the day-to-day tactics than the big-picture vision that we all get excited about.

"With that one simple question, we feel like we all have a say in the matter," Mark says. "We feel like we can control our own destiny. We don't feel like we're walking off the plank into the strategic idea of the month. And more importantly, we're not blindly guiding our fearless leader astray, either."

There are a few chuckles in the room, with more head nods.

"With this approach, we work together as a team and as one unit," Mark says. "We can all row together in the same boat."

Mark finally sits back in his chair. What feels like an incredibly long silence fills the room as we all digest what he says.

To me, this feels like the *Jerry Maguire* movie with Tom Cruise. In the film, he's stayed up all night to write a memo about how sports agents are doing things wrong called, "The Things We Think and Do Not Say." He makes copies for everyone at the tradeshow — then freaks out after he realizes he made a mistake. He rushes to the lobby to get rid of the memos, only to realize he's too late.

Breaking the silence in the room, Sandy starts to clap. Mike joins in, and soon everyone else is clapping for Mark.

"Finally," Mike says. "Someone says it."

I feel a mix of emotions at that moment: I'm elated that there's this level of engagement in the process, and that my team has the courage to talk about the hard things. At the same time, I feel some déjà vu.

In the next scene, Jerry Maguire loses his job after writing the memo.

Oh, great, I think to myself. *I'm going to lose my controller too.*

Chapter 24

Defining the Oars

Spurred by Mike's speech, everyone dives into the "how" portion of the retreat with vigor. We took a 30-minute break after the applause died down, then came back to the conference room to start working on each of the three journeys, one by one.

I map out each journey on our whiteboard:

Journey #1 — Increase sales from outbound team

Oar #1: Realign current sales team's respective industries and territories within two months

Oar #2: Hire two new sales team members within six months

Oar #3: Train current sales team members to create $200,000 incremental sales within 12 months

Journey #2 — Add production capacity to scale with company growth

Oar #1: Increase production capacity to 80% effectiveness within nine months

Oar #2: Purchase tool to automate manual cutting within 12 months

Oar #3: Expand to swing shift within 18 months (as production capacity is needed)

Journey #3 — Increase recurring sales by existing customers

Oar #1: Analyze trends with top 20% of customers within two months

Oar #2: Market trends toward next 20% of customers within eight months

Oar #3: Train inside sales team to take initiative within 12 months

"This is great," Sandy says. "But it looks like we've already completed the 'how' for each one."

She has a good point. There's a lot of detail in the lists. But before I can respond, Mark jumps in.

"I agree with you to a certain extent," he says. "But there's still so much more to do. Let's take a look."

He gestures for the whiteboard marker, and I toss it over to him.

"Look at oar #1 for our journey #1," Mark says. "It doesn't say who's going to do it. It doesn't say what the new territories are going to be, or what method we'll use to realign them to the appropriate sales staff. It just says 'within two months.'"

Mark is really on a roll today.

"I agree," Mike hops in. "There are so many details for what needs to happen in order to implement these. You have to figure out what the territories are going to be. You need to get buy-in from all the parties involved. You need to make sure our customers are happy with the changes. You need to change the territories in the CRM system. You need to change them in the accounting system, so we can pay commissions. Actually, you may want to evaluate a change in the commission policy to support all this too..."

Sandy puts her hand up.

"Okay, okay, I get it," she says, laughing. "Frankly, it's all those little details that drive me crazy. No wonder it's important to be patient with this process."

I jump back in, as much as I love seeing how animated everyone is to get this stuff done.

"Every great company — every ship — needs the whole picture of where it's headed," I say. "It needs vision. It needs to know the destination of where it's headed. It needs clarification about the journey it will need to take to get there. And it needs oars: the power to make it happen. Without all these working together, the ship doesn't sail as fast as it could. I really believe we're on the right track now with all those pieces."

I look up at the clock on the wall. *How are we already to the last hour of this retreat?* It's been an emotional — but effective — 48 hours. The mood in the room feels triumphant, but I can tell from all the yawns going around the table that everyone is about ready to head home too.

"Okay, so what's next?" Sandy asks.

Charlie has already coached me on this next step. In his estimation, this step could make or break the momentum we've spent all this time building. Sure, there are tons of ideas — and plans — bouncing around this conference room. But as soon as we get back to the office, there needs to be immediate action. We need quick wins.

"In three weeks, I need all three journey leaders to report back on where they are," I say. "You'll need to meet with your respective teams and get any cross-functional buy-in that you need. Your goal over the next three weeks will be to complete the 'oars' for each journey. What are going to be the tactics, the power, that you'll need in order to complete your journey?"

I pull up my computer and put everyone's email address on a calendar invite for three weeks from that day: Oar Review.

"You'll need to schedule your first meeting with your team within a week," I say, already knowing what the reaction is about to be.

I'm met almost immediately by annoyed glances, followed by multiple people jumping in at once with their excuses for why this timeline won't work: travel, other commitments, someone was out sick last week.

"I'm serious about this," I say, holding up my hand to pause the complaints.

Sandy chimes back in.

"Well, to continue the ship metaphor, we're kind of heading back into the storm now," she says. "It's easy to return to our day-to-day actions just to stay afloat — and then not actually move forward. But we've got to stay focused and lead strategically. We can't give up this momentum we've built."

Everyone nods. It's easy to recognize how much work they've accomplished over the past two days: and no one wanted to lose that work by getting sucked back into the chaos of the day-to-day.

I smile a little too much. Sandy has shown really great leadership this weekend. It's not always easy to step up and say what's obvious — especially when it's not exactly the most popular belief. No one *really* wanted to schedule more meetings with their teams all within a week. But it's clear we need to if we're going to actually accomplish *any* of what we've outlined this weekend.

"Here's my side of the commitment," I say, remembering that the team has (rightly) called me out a couple of times this weekend for not staying accountable. "I've already scheduled an all-hands meeting on Tuesday of this upcoming week when we return to the office. I plan to review with the whole company our vision and destination. I'll mention at that meeting that the next step of the process is they'll all meet with their individual team leaders to finish up the journeys and map out the 'oars.' I really want to convey to them that you all will need their guidance. Nothing is final. We'll review feedback from anyone who wants to provide it, and we'll adjust from there."

"This time will be different," I say. "And you'll feel the difference."

Still, in the back of my mind, I can't help but feel a little smidge of doubt. I haven't yet figured out what to do about Mike leaving — which is quite the wrench in these plans. As a start, I'm planning to meet with Mike and all the other key departmental leaders and supervisors on Monday. We'll do a broader email announcement by the end of that day, then make time for an all-hands Q&A meeting.

Mark raises his hand.

"So, what are we going to do in three weeks?" he asks. "And what will we do after that?"

I catch myself before I openly sigh in frustration. *Didn't I just say that?* I think to myself.

I think back to my old university professor, who said that people were only paying attention to what you said one-third of the time. So if something is important, repeat it three times.

"Okay, so in three weeks, we'll have all the destination leaders report back on the status of their journeys and what the supporting oars will need to be to get the job done," I answer. "You'll get an example document of this in your email inbox by Monday. You can use this as a template to fill in your own answers."

I pull up an example PDF on my screen, which is still connected to the projector in the room.

"This is what I'll be sending to all the journey leaders," I say. "We'll have a 'Trim' meeting where we'll go over all the most important components of the strategic plan. Is everyone clear with their responsibilities?"

Mark raises his hand again.

"I'm not assigned to anything specific," he says. "What should I be doing?"

"Oh, thank you for asking, Mark," I say. "I almost forgot. And this is particularly important. Your job is to gather resource requests for each of the strategic elements. Whether it's recent sales team members, a second shift, a new tool. Incorporate all these items within the one-year budget and three-year forecast."

I can't believe I'd almost forgotten one of the most important elements Charlie had conveyed to me: the strategic plan needs to tie directly into the budget and financial forecast. A huge percentage of strategic initiatives never get tied back to the budget, he'd told me. So no wonder nothing ever gets done. If something isn't in the budget, no one gets approval for the critical decisions they need to make in order to actually accomplish anything.

Secondly, I want to make sure there's accountability in our strategic investments. In the past, we've tended to spend whatever we needed to get something done if we thought it was important. And then as a result, we'd miss our bottom line, because we had been underestimating the money or time it would take to get something done.

This time is going to be different, I repeat in my head.

"This leads me to my next point," I say. "Include some buffer into your estimates for how long you think it'll take to complete your projects. Any time you're dealing with implementing a new project, there's always some uncertainty. As we move forward with these projects, we'll be holding one another accountable to get them done in a timely manner. But this should be based on a buffered timeline, not a perfect or ideal world."

I look around the room. "Does anyone remember the last time we finished a strategic plan on time? Or finished it at all?"

By the uncomfortable shifting in their chairs, I can tell everyone already knows the answer. Nobody raises their hand.

"Exactly," I say. "I want to avoid this in the future. We're not going to be perfect, but with our new approach, we should have much more success than we've had in the past."

"Now," I continue. "When you add in your buffers, use reasonable judgment."

"Does that mean that everyone should add 10 percent more time to their timeline, 20 percent, 30 percent...?" Mark trails off.

"We should be adding the right amount of buffer to make sure we have an 80 to 90 percent confidence rate of achieving our first-year journeys," I answer. "For longer-term journeys, we want to add in enough buffer to where we have about 70 percent confidence of success. This isn't absolute, but that's a general rule to follow."

"I know we also talked about stretch destinations," I continued. "We 'expect' to miss those. We're not going to be perfect in pursuing everything we want to accomplish. However, if we communicate that those stretch destinations are committed goals, then there's going to be less tolerance for missing those targets. Still, there's going to be some risk of failure. When we have multiple uncertain targets, there will always be some risk of failure. We have to be willing to accept that."

Mark frowns. I can tell he's struggling a bit with this piece. He wants perfection — an exact formula. A debit = a credit.

But I can't provide him with that. Maybe I have a long-term problem at that position, I think to myself. I need a controller in that seat who is willing to accept some risk — especially if we're going to reach for more "stretch" destinations and really grow this company to what it's capable of.

The telltale sound of zippers and the rustle of papers as people pack up their bags fills the room. I know half the room is just ready to go back home and see their families. But the other half is intrigued by the conversation.

"So, how do you measure success?" Mark asks.

Now *that* is a great question. And it gets everyone's attention — enough to where everyone stops zipping up their backpacks.

"I know we thought we were going to leave 30 minutes early, but this question is worth reviewing," I say. "Does everyone have time to talk through this?"

Everyone nods their heads.

"Great," I say. "Okay, take your notebooks out really quick. Write down how you think we should measure success for this strategic plan. I'll give you a few minutes, and then we'll review."

About ten minutes go by, as the whole team continues to scribble on their pads.

I go back to the whiteboard one more time to write out everyone's ideas as they call them out:

- *Complete 100% of our journeys*
- *Meet our financial budget*
- *Complete 70% of our journeys*
- *High employee engagement with the strategic plan*
- *Complete our key destination in 3 years*
- *Complete 70% of our key journeys in 3 years*

- *Be on track for 10-year vision by the end of 3 years*
- *Reaching $20 million in sales in 3 years*
- *Finding sales personnel to help us hit our financial goals*
- *Increasing company value*
- *Meet or exceed bottom line target for 1 and 3 years*
- *Obtain friendly investor in 3 years*
- *Highest NPS scores in the industry*
- *Scale production to meet growth*
- *Maintain high quality with growth*
- *Improve on-time delivery rate to 95%*
- *Employee turnover is the lowest in the industry*
- *Leading provider of products and services in the industry*

When I hear someone call out that last one, I have to stop myself from rolling my eyes. If I had a nickel for every time I've read that a company was the leading this or leading that... I'd be a millionaire. Ironically, this whole process should theoretically... help me become a millionaire. Hmm.

Admittedly, I don't feel totally ready to lead *this* brainstorming session. Charlie and I had talked about KPIs a bit — but not enough to where I feel equipped to take this list and actually turn it into something actionable. So, I punt.

"This is an impressive list," I say, turning back to the table. "It's clearly something we'll have to get clarity on before we officially start executing on our plan. We have to identify what the most important measures of success are, and how we can keep them top of mind. This will be a process that we can pick back up with when we're back in the office."

I hate ending this retreat on a question — and with ambiguity. But rushing through this, especially when everyone was on the verge of heading home just 15 minutes ago, doesn't feel right either.

Sandy steps in.

"Jack," she says. "I've been collaborating with you for the past five years. We've had some great difficulties and challenges as we've tried to navigate our way through this messy world."

I nod my head, thinking back to all the chaos of the past couple years.

"We've done these planning sessions in the past," she says. "And as you know, most haven't always added value. But this was different. The answers weren't pre-determined, and I felt like everyone really contributed. People were engaged. And it feels like we have a lot of hope and optimism moving forward. Thank you for leading us through this."

She starts to clap again — but this time for me.

Everyone else joins in, and Sandy surprises me by getting up to give me a hug. Mike comes over and puts his arm around my shoulders. Dan and Nancy each give me a high-five. Mark stays in his chair but flashes a thumbs-up.

I'm surprised to feel a tiny prick of tears behind my eyes.

What in the Sam Hill? I think. *What is going on with all this emotion?*

I can't say anything for a moment, but finally manage a "Thank you."

With that, everyone grabs their stuff and heads toward the door to get back to their families for the rest of the weekend.

Before I do the same, I take a moment to stand alone in the empty room. Sticky notes still plaster the walls and table, and our whiteboards are still full of scribbles. I start to have a little hope too as I look around at all the ideas and plans we've accumulated in such a short time.

I look down at my phone before I start to clean up — a text from Charlie: *How did it go?*

But first, I have to call my wife.

Chapter 25

Coaching the Retreat

"I told you so," Monica says as soon as I finish telling her about the retreat — and Mike's expected departure.

She's right. She has somewhat of a sixth sense and always seems to know what's really going on beneath the surface. And she's been predicting for months (maybe even years) that Mike was on his way out. I always have my head down when it comes to people's emotions, just trying to get things done, so sometimes I miss the forest for the trees. Monica never does, though.

She asks me to pick up a few things from the grocery store on the way home, and I figure it's the least I can do. About ten minutes into my drive, Charlie calls me.

"How did it go?" he asks.

I start rambling — and don't stop for the next ten minutes. Besides the recap I gave to Monica, I haven't been able to talk to anyone at this point about Mike's impending departure — and what the heck I'm going to do.

Still, I want to celebrate the victories, especially since Charlie played such a role in helping us have such a successful strategic retreat. We probably *still* would be having some meandering discussion about a goal that's not even that likely, if not for Charlie's structure.

I tell Charlie about how engaged the team was, how much we got done, all the journeys we'd picked out and planned together, and then that pesky final question...

"So, how *do* we measure success?" I ask.

"Well…" Charlie trails off, choosing his next words carefully. "You and your team have to define success. If I tell you what success is, will that actually feel fulfilling? Success has to be something that's hard to reach, but also provides a sense of significant accomplishment when you get there. Only you and the people in the trenches with you will know what that looks like for your company."

"Now, from a pure strategic planning perspective, I can help you define some benchmarks," Charlie continues. "But remember, we can't get to the results, without focusing on what we *need to do* to get there."

"So you're saying we need to measure some of those actions?"

"Exactly. Measuring things you can actually control is the only way you'll know that you're actually on track to reach your vision. So 80 percent of your measurements should be Key Performance Indicators that are *leading* behaviors: things you have control over. The other 20 percent can be about lagging results: things you don't have direct control over, like sales numbers. Sales numbers are the end result, determined by a customer's action, not yours."

I nod my head, deep in thought, and try not to drive off the road. My brain is going about a thousand miles an hour. The KPIs our team has always measured have been those lagging ones — sales figures, revenue, all the data that doesn't come in until the end of a quarter or the end of a year. But I see what Charlie is saying here: we should be measuring all the actions *leading up* to those numbers, if we hope to actually make regular progress.

"A big mistake I see organizations make is they assume there is only one silver bullet solution," Charlie says. "An organization will bet on one thing, one strategy, to win the game. The problem is that everything is constantly changing: the organization itself, customers, vendors, systems, economics, employees, politics, the environment, competitors. Business isn't a game of checkers — it's more like chess. We may try something we think will work, but all those fluctuating factors can lead to an unexpected response. Which changes the way we have to do things internally. A strategy needs some flexibility to actually make a difference and get the effect you want. And just because you've tried a strategy at another organization that may look or feel exactly like where you are now, it doesn't mean it'll work again with your current employees, or your location, or the systems, or anything else."

"That makes sense," I agree. "Kind of like companies that had successful strategies work before, but then when COVID struck, all of that pretty much went out the door. The environment you're operating in is constantly changing."

"Yep," Charlie says. "So you should have multiple strategies that increase your likelihood of success. We need to analyze the true cause and effect. So when a strategy isn't working, we can let it go. Or sometimes you realize that you need to pair one strategy with another. Or a strategy needs to be spearheaded by a different leader. A different combination can be the difference between success and failure."

"So this is why the 'trim' stage of my strategy is so important. You need to cut the fat and get rid of what's not working. You need to ask yourself: 'Is this strategy truly having an impact on the outcome? Is this the right combination of strategies? Do we have enough resources to make this successful? Are we going to have enough patience to see if the strategy will provide results, or do we need to pivot to something that will have quicker results?' Challenge your team to answer these questions truthfully. And remember: Strategy planning is a hypothesis, not a fact."

Now, this is a concept I've never really thought about. In all my decades of experience, I've always taken a pretty hard line approach to a strategic plan: *Here's the plan. Get it done. Don't deviate from the plan.*

But what Charlie is saying makes sense. No strategic plan should be locked into place like that. It needs to flex and move alongside everything else happening — both at the organization and in the world.

If I've learned anything over the past couple years of pandemic, inflation, supply chain chaos, political turmoil, and everything else happening… It's that some flexibility can make a huge difference.

"So, starting any journey with 100 percent confidence is usually the wrong move," Charlie says. "That is a fixed mindset, mixed with a bit of arrogance. We need to have a learning mindset. If there are immovable objects in our way, we need to adjust our bearings. Maybe lift our anchor when an unexpected wind stirs up, and it looks like it could move us in the right direction."

"How would I know if the wind is going to take us in the right direction, though?" I ask.

"By paying attention to the buoys," Charlie answers. "You need some indicators in your path to help you see whether you're heading the right way or not. So let's go back to the original question: How do you measure success? You should absolutely be measuring whether you reach the destination you want. But that's not the only way to measure success. You also need to measure success based on the leading indicators we talked about. You need to measure how the journey is going, not just whether you've arrived at your end destination. You need to keep track of whether you're following your buoys."

"How often should we be doing that?"

"Quarterly and monthly, for sure. But also weekly. You need to learn to love the process of getting there, not just arriving. Think about this: We see interviews and read articles about successful entrepreneurs, actors, and athletes. The press will ask, 'What allowed you to sell your company, or win that Oscar, or win the championship?' This is often kind of a silly question. Because on the outside, we may see the entrepreneur netting millions of dollars after selling their startup to a larger company. But it took 12 years to build that business. Or we'll watch a 30-second acceptance speech from an actor after a 15-year career. Or we see the winning touchdown thrown by the famous quarterback. It took Michael Jordan seven seasons before he won his first ring with the Chicago Bulls. Was there really *one* action before those moments that created that success?"

I think back to the scene of my favorite NFL quarterback, ten years deep into his career, throwing that winning touchdown pass a few weeks ago. Sure, that was one moment. But it took years of work to be able to throw a pass like that.

"If you think about all these examples, there was a lot more that went into those moments than the end result that we saw from the outside," Charlie continues. "For the CEO, was it the sale… or was it the consistency the CEO had displayed in adding value to the marketplace for 12 years? For the actor, was it the movie… or was it the tireless work of practicing lines in a script or taking acting classes? For the quarterback, was it really that final throw? Or was it the hours of practicing that throwing motion nearly every day since he was 12 years old? For Michael Jordan, was it the game-winning shot or the hours of relentless practice?"

"That stuff really does take such a long time to perfect," I agree.

"I'll ask this too," Charlie says. "Why does a CEO return to a new company, even after earning enough money to never have to work again, from the sale of her first one? Why does an actor try another film even after winning the Oscar? Why does a quarterback keep playing even after winning multiple Super Bowls? It's clearly not just about the results. Because CEOs don't sell a new business every year. Actors don't win Oscars for every movie. And even Tom Brady has failed to win a Super Bowl in two-thirds of his career. Why did Michael Jordan come back to basketball after winning three championships and playing professional baseball?"

My eyebrows raise a little when he puts it like this. He's right.

"Are you in this for the process or the results?" Charlie continues. "The greatest at their craft are usually the ones who love the process, just as much as the satisfaction of having won. The best, most sustainable leaders are in it for both. They love the results, of course. But they love the process, too. A

CEO who only focuses on results, without loving the process on the way there, may get their prize. But it will usually come at a cost."

"I've seen plenty of CEOs around my age go through that," I admit, thinking of all the divorced dads I know who may have sold their company — but missed out on a lot of time with their families.

"The best leaders are the ones who celebrate the small AND the big wins," Charlie says. "They recognize success is in the thousands of little decisions and habits that contributed to the big win at the end. It's those leaders who have the patience to stay in it to really win in the end."

"So, Jack. How do you measure success?"

I pause, as the trees flash by my driver's side window.

Charlie's right, even if he isn't speaking about me specifically. I've been so focused on earning the reward that everything else has become subservient to it. And when I've been blasted with the challenges of the past couple years, and the destination feels further and further away, I get more and more frustrated with work.

I cringe a little when I think about the number of times someone on the team would drop into my office and say that a strategy wasn't working — and I just ignored them. Instead, I would reply with, "I don't care how you get there. Just get me results."

The results wouldn't happen, which would just drive even more frustration.

Too often, I focus solely on delivering results — which I've been great at for years. Sometimes, it almost seemed easy.

But life is different when you're at the top of a complex organization in an even-more-complex, ever-changing environment. There are so many variables and things that aren't directly in my control.

I'm realizing now that failing to learn from those challenges — and failing to appreciate the small victories along the way — is just driving my frustration. Maybe it's even hurting my effectiveness too.

But Charlie is helping me see this isn't a sustainable strategy. Having tunnel vision and only seeing the end destination is a recipe for disaster — or at least a lot more frustration when things don't go according to plan. Which, now that I think about it, is pretty much always.

I have to change the way I work, or I'm going to be miserable for a long time. There's a better way to lead. And there's a better way to work.

"You need to start measuring victories in smaller increments," Charlie says, interrupting my train of thought. "Because think about it: will straight up winning actually create more joy?"

"Well, not necessarily," I say, thinking back to my younger days. "There have definitely been times I've been a winner but not felt happy. Usually, it was because I hated the people I was playing with. My junior year baseball team had the best record of my whole career — but the captain was a real jerk and made playing on the team pretty miserable. Even at work, it's always been about the people around me. At my first job at a fast-food restaurant, the manager was always yelling at someone. In one of my first jobs out of college at a textile company, the GM didn't care about me at all. All he cared about were results."

I gulp a little as I say this. I'm starting to see a little too much of myself in that old manager.

Wait...

Is Mike leaving because of me?

Most people leave their jobs because of their managers.

Is our turnover high because of what I'm doing as CEO? Aren't I responsible at the end of the day for the people we hire... and then how we manage them?

How do I create a team where everyone will celebrate the win... and actually stick around to see it happen? What type of leader do I want to be?

And why am I not considering that leadership in the strategic plan?

I feel anxiety bubble up into my chest.

In a bit of a panic, I ask, "Is it okay to add this into the strategy?"

"Will this help you measure success?" Charlie asks. "Will your actions create a winning team, but also an engaged, happy team? If so, then focusing on your leadership could have an impact on the results you get."

"So how do I go about doing this now? What do I need to do?"

"Remember how I said you need a 'trim' stage for your strategic plan? That phase is all about making sure you have all the key elements for success. Your leadership — and how you communicate what winning looks like within the organization — is a huge piece of that."

"How do I make sure I'm presenting the strategic plan in that way?" I ask. "How can I get everyone on board?"

"Are you in a place where you can take a couple of notes?" Charlie asks.

Well, I am now, I think. I pull off an exit ramp and park at the grocery store right off the exit.

"Yeah, go for it," I say.

"Okay, so each destination, journey, and oar statement should stand on its own," Charlie says. "Make sure each statement has all the following elements."

I scribble down each one Charlie says:

- *One clear, action-oriented sentence*
- *Each statement is trying to accomplish one thing.*
- *First word of each sentence should be an action word*
- *Each statement should have a captain or leader who's solely responsible for its success. It's okay to have multiple people supporting the statement, but there should be one clear leader*
- *Start date and end date*
- *A measurement to define success.*

"You need to write each piece with clarity," Charlie continues. "Your 12-year-old niece or nephew should be able to read and understand what's happening. I've had the privilege of working with some of the most intelligent people in their professions: practicing physicians, PhDs in their respective fields, attorneys, engineers, successful entrepreneurs. And one thing they have in common is they have a tendency to overcomplicate the simple. Don't fall down that rabbit hole. Keep the statements so clear that everyone in the organization can understand exactly what they mean.

"You can write a short supporting paragraph to describe the statements in more detail. But keep them snappy. If there's ambiguity, remove it. Now, remember that you're working on something new that you may not have experienced before. So there's uncertainty. But don't confuse uncertainty with a lack of clarity on what you're trying to accomplish."

"Let me ask you something, especially since you've been driving for most of this call," Charlie says. "Have you ever driven in really thick fog? What do you do when you can't see clearly?"

"Well, I usually slow down, or if it's really thick, sometimes I'll just stop completely," I answer.

"Exactly. Writing unclear statements creates fog for your team. So they won't move forward quickly. They may even stop completely if they're unclear as to where they're going and what they're trying to accomplish."

This all clicks in my head. I think back to the hundreds — if not thousands — of times I've fired off an unclear email, voicemail, or verbal request.

I roll my eyes a little at myself. I've even made *strategic plans* that were unclear.

I tend to think my team knows exactly what they're supposed to do, just because they nod in agreement. But then a few days later, I'll ask how it's going, and they'll say they don't fully understand what they're supposed to be doing. Or worse, they've already started, and they've gone in a completely wrong direction, wasting their time — and our resources. Then we have to unwind all those efforts.

And that kind of thing happens *way* more often than I'd like. The worst part is that those team members are usually doing their best — and then get in trouble when I come in and tell them they're doing it wrong, when I didn't even tell them how to do it correctly in the first place!

This is really hard, I think.

"Yes, we make our life harder by not doing it right," Charlie responds. I'm surprised to hear him responding, because I'd thought I'd just said that part to myself.

"What do you mean by not doing it right?" I ask.

"Well, you need to be principle-based when you create your strategic plan," Charlie says. "There are seven principles that I take all my strategy clients through. And you have to follow them in order, because skipping over any one of them could sink your ship. We've already talked about the first four. Your Compass stage — that's your vision. The Aspire step — that's setting your destinations. Then there's Plan — that one's self-explanatory. It's your strategic retreat, and mapping out all your journeys and oars. Then it's the Trim phase, where you're focusing on the most important pieces of your business that will get you where you want to go. Next is the fifth stage. And this one's all about *starting.* People will build strategic plans every year. But they'll never actually get started on them. Why do you think that is, Jack?"

I'm at a loss for words. If I knew the answer to that, our company probably would have made a *lot* more progress over the last several years.

"Let's start from the beginning," Charlie says. "If you develop a plan that doesn't have a sharp vision, your team will rarely follow through. If you don't set clear destinations, people aren't clear about where they're going. If you don't develop a clear plan, they won't know how to get there. And if you don't trim the plan, your team won't know how to prioritize what comes next."

"That all makes sense," I agree.

"Only 20 percent of organizations start their strategic plans on time," Charlie adds. "Usually, it's because they haven't properly worked through those first four steps. But the second reason for the late start is they're afraid. Change is difficult. CEOs are used to rewarding managers for keeping the ship running. Rarely are managers rewarded for changing the status quo — and rocking that boat."

"So, how do you flip that mindset?" I ask.

"Managers need a *compelling* reason to change," Charlie says. "Research shows that 51 percent of managers will fight change. More than half! But if you can help those same managers see how they can be a part of a new future — and how that new future actually benefits them — they're more likely to fight *for* you instead of against you."

"A good starting point," Charlie continues, "is making the first action step really easy. As your team gets ready to tackle the first oar, make it easy. Develop some early confidence. And the other important piece to this is creating *clear start dates* — and then realistic end dates. Set an up-front expectation that there will be accountability to adhere to those dates."

"Yeah, it's amazing how often we forget to put in an actual start date," I say, thinking back to all those prior strategic plans… which never actually happened. "We only ever set end dates."

"You're exactly right — and you're not alone," Charlie says. "So many companies fall into the same trap. So make sure there's clarity over what everyone needs to do first. Once you create that clarity, it helps propel your team forward in the right direction."

"That really is a huge piece that we've been missing," I agree.

"Jack, have you ever read *Good to Great*? It's by Jim Collins," Charlie asks.

I say I haven't.

"One of my favorite stories from that book is a story about Walgreens," Charlie says. "Cork Walgreen and the rest of the management team had made the decision to get rid of the famous Corky's stores that were named after him. And they decided it was going to be a five-year plan. Six months after they'd decided to move forward, Corky overheard someone on the leadership team mentioning that they had five years to get rid of the stores. Corky interrupted them to say, 'No, you have four and a half years to do it.' It was that clarity and accountability from leadership that helped propel the executive team to action. Now, for the small to midsize businesses I usually work with, six months is way too long to wait."

"Agreed," I say. "We definitely need to move faster than that with some of these initiatives."

"Don't forget fear," Charlie adds. "People are afraid to fail. Strategy is a process of trying something new to reach a new destination; therefore, there is risk of failure. Rarely will all of our journeys and oars work. We need to foster a culture where we accept that failure is learning what we should *not* be doing. And this is a good thing."

"Oh, it's almost time for me to go," Charlie says. "Remember one other thing: your team members are continuously evaluating you to see how serious you are on different initiatives. They think you'll read the next management book, jump onto the latest fad, and just forget about the initiatives you've laid out. Change that mindset. Keep them accountable and moving forward — and don't just let your strategies be fads that everyone forgets about."

With that last statement hanging overhead, we hang up. There are so many thoughts swirling in my head, I can't even remember what I'm supposed to pick up at the grocery. Now, *that's* a strategy my wife will tell you I almost always forget.

Chapter 26

Working Toward Clarity

By the time I get to the office, I'm halfway expecting the team to have already forgotten their roles in the next piece of the strategy: Huddle with their teams and figure out their individual journeys — and the oars to power them through.

But everyone turns their documents in on time, and I'm really impressed. All the managers have already met with their teams, gotten feedback, and even made changes to what they turned in. I know that's the kind of agility we're going to need moving forward.

It's time to start trimming, though. I'm nervous about what this meeting will bring. Everyone's (rightfully) attached to their ideas and plans — but I know our chances of success are going to be so much higher if we can narrow in on the most impactful and most likely to happen.

As we sit down in the conference room to start trimming down our strategic plan, I slide a box of donuts onto the table. I know at least one person might appreciate my "dad joke" about eating something fatty while we trim the fat.

Sandy speaks up first as she grabs a chocolate glazed.

"Well, I have to admit I wasn't really looking forward to going through this exercise, despite how great I felt after the retreat," she says. "But my team gave some great input, and they helped me see things I didn't expect, and they were really engaged. Some people were a little concerned about the growth plan, but overall there was a real feeling of excitement from the whole team that they were going to be part of a growing organization. And of course, growth means more commissions, so that was really compelling to them."

"They were also really helpful with coming up with some new ideas and helping me understand what kind of skills we should be looking for in the hiring process," she continues. "And I got some good insights about how we should consider the territory realignment. We didn't settle on any firm answers, of course, but we definitely got a little bit of a head start, which was really positive."

"You know, the only problem I had with my group was I got called a 'short-timer' about 58 times," Mike says.

Everyone in the room chuckles a little at this. The email about his departure had gone out, and the news had surprised most people — but they understood his reasoning.

"There was actually a lot of real excitement from the team," Mike says. "They're seeing opportunities of what they can do and how they can add some innovative ideas to help expand capacity. Actually, they think we might not even need to add a second shift yet. They think we could be more effective by just tweaking the current process. There are some areas of waste with how we're doing things now, and if we could eliminate those spots, we could probably expand capacity without actually needing to add the extra shift."

"Wow, that's great," I say, surprised — but impressed — at how quickly Mike's team was able to find all the holes in the production process. It's impossible to know if it'll work yet. But it's worth a shot.

"I know this isn't what we had originally thought about, but would you be okay if we tried those steps first to see if we can increase our productivity without getting that second shift set up?" I ask. "Because that would be brilliant — and potentially huge savings if we could push that out."

"Yeah, let's do it that way," Mike says. "If we can eliminate these non-value activities in the process, I think we can get rid of a lot of wasted time. By moving products through faster, we should be able to ship more products with the same resources."

"That's music to my ears," I say.

Mike smiles. "You know, Jack..." he says. "I'm really excited about what's ahead. I know you are searching for a replacement, but I'm considering staying on — maybe in a different role supporting these changes and helping the team to implement them — if you'll have me."

I look around the table to make sure everyone else just heard what I heard. I can't believe it. In my head, I've already moved on past Mike — what other choice did I have? But here was potentially a fantastic opportunity to keep someone on who knew a lot about our current systems and could help with the transition.

"Mike, are you serious?" I ask.

"Yeah, I really am," he says. "See, when we initially talked about shipping more products, all I thought about was working more hours. I knew that wasn't going to fly for me at home. But then I talked to Kenny, our materials' assembly tech. He was part of a lean manufacturing team with a different organization before he came here — and honestly I'd always kind of ignored him, because he always had a lot of questions. I would usually just tell him to get back to work. But during our departmental strategy meeting, he talked about finding better ways to ship, using one-piece flow, and eliminating waste. Initially, I didn't give him the time of day. But then he shared specific examples on our current shop floor of how we could really improve. Kenny's been with our team for two years, and he's been an incredible resource this whole time. I just never let him speak. He told me this week he had been ready to accept another offer until he heard about some of these new strategy goals. I think he and I are both in the same boat. We're excited about working smarter, not harder. This new methodology really gives us hope. It gives me hope, at least. I think I could contribute in a different role, with some different responsibilities."

Another day, another surprise, I think. Mike really could be a huge help as we get some of these initiatives going…

Someone who I have a little more doubt about, though, is Mark, our controller. As we move past Mike's announcement, Mark stays quiet. He hardly contributes anything to the discussion for the entire 90 minutes, other than to say he's collected everyone's financial information already and is working on resource allocations.

Well, at least there's that, I think.

We move on to some of the journey statements that everyone's come up with. But this is where I start to get a little concerned — most of the statements aren't clear guidelines. They don't include KPIs — or buoys, as Charlie calls them.

I hold my hand up and pause the meeting.

"This next part we're going to work on today is going to be difficult because we have to really dive into the details," I say. "We want to make sure everyone in the company clearly understands exactly what's being said. We want them to know exactly the destination, which journeys we are using to get there, and how our oars are going to move us in the direction. We have to remove any ambiguity as much as we can. I know we won't be able to get through all this today, but I do want to make sure we get this done the right way. Let's take a look at the first journey, and the oars that will power that journey. Here, Sandy, why don't you walk us through your statements from your perspective. You can hook up your laptop to the big screen."

I toss her the cord, and she gets everything set up on the screen as we wait.

As her document flashes onto the screen, she scrolls to the "journey" section.

We start walking through them one by one, going piece by piece. Is there a start date? An end date? Does the objective include one clear sentence, or does it have extra filler content? Is there a captain for each one? Are there KPIs listed, and do they make sense for their specific strategies?

The whole process is time-consuming and tedious. But I try to keep everyone's heads up, and remind them that this is all part of our foundation. And once we have this strong foundation built, everything else gets easier from here.

By the time we get through a few rounds of this for Sandy's objective statements, we're starting to get the hang of it. After comparing the first draft with the second, everyone agrees there's a lot more clarity.

"Team, we're going to have to do this with every statement," I say. "Since we can't get through all of them in this meeting, you and your teams will have to reconvene and get these squared away. How about a week for everyone to review and get back with your updates?"

Nancy raises her hand. "Jack," she says. "We're already a week behind."

"We are," I say. "I'd rather wait two weeks to launch the strategic plan in confidence rather than launch today with confusion."

Everyone nods. Heck, they remember the past few years too, when everyone was confused about their roles and responsibilities. No one wants a repeat.

"I'm trying out this new thing called patience," I say, drawing another chuckle. Everyone knows how much that characteristic has *not* been a part of the process in past years' strategic plans.

"Jack, I have another question before we go," Sandy says as everyone starts packing up their laptops and grabbing the last of the donuts for the road. "We need more data to intelligently design the sales territories and product mix."

"Hey Mark, would you be able to help Sandy with that analysis?"

"Uh…" he says, as he shuffles some papers on the table. "I guess I can do that."

I can tell he's reluctant — but at least he agrees.

I'm not sure how much of a problem Mark is going to be moving forward. But at least everyone else seems ready to roll. Within a week, we'll have the revised destinations, journeys, and oars. Everything will have measurements, designated captains, and start and end dates.

Now we're really ready to start sailing.

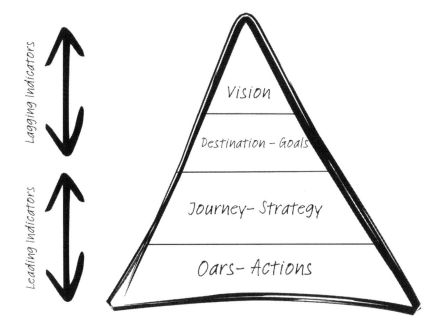

Chapter 27

Starting the Journey

Three weeks later, we have a regular leadership meeting on the calendar, and it's time to review our strategy spreadsheet.

Since we finalized all the journey and oar statements, we've dumped everything into a spreadsheet, with a column to the right side for comments. Soon enough, we realize that's not going to be enough, especially since our limited meeting time doesn't really leave us enough time to go over everyone's comments or dig into significant questions. So we devise a color code system for the spreadsheet: Green means the project is on track. Yellow means it's running behind. And a red project is on hold.

The visual indicator is helpful to keep a bird's-eye view over everything. And within a couple of weeks, I'm starting to see the problems pile up. The yellow flags are starting to increase, and there are even a couple of red flags already. Usually everyone's excuse is they're too busy with their day-to-day responsibilities, and the pieces of the strategic plan just feel like something else on their plates.

At our next strategy meeting, I ask Sandy why she's thrown a red flag onto one of her journeys.

"It was green just a couple of weeks ago," I say.

Mark interrupts before Sandy can say anything.

"I can tell you why," he says. "Sandy put in a request to hire two new people, and she decided to use recruiters to hire them. I'd heard someone talking about this in the lunchroom, so I investigated a little and saw that the total comp planned for these new sales personnel, plus the percentage that would go to the recruiter, would exceed the planned expenses for the whole quarter. So I told Sandy they can't use the recruiters to hire the new folks."

With a frown, Sandy jumps in.

"Yeah, and this has completely stonewalled the hiring process," she says. "Without the recruiters, there's no way we can hit the timeline to hire the salespeople we need on the timeline we have outlined here."

"So what's your next step, Sandy?" I ask.

And here was Mark again…

"If we want to hit our bottom-line numbers, we're going to have to pay attention to our expenses compared to the plan," he interrupts again. "This applies to everyone on the team."

Sandy leans forward in her chair and is opening and closing her mouth, trying to get in a word as Mark talks about expenses. She's visibly upset now.

I ask her again, "What's your next step here?"

"Well, I don't know," she says, rolling her eyes in frustration. "What can I do?"

Everyone seems to have a thought about that. Over the next 15 minutes, we argue over all the different options: hire both people now? Hire one now, and another later? Recruit candidates in some other way?

It's clear that to focus on specific industries the way we have outlined in our strategic plan, we need to hire new salespeople to fill the gap. And more importantly, that extra staff will build up our incremental sales — pretty much a linchpin of this strategy.

"What if we completed an analysis on the three-year benefit of hiring the second salesperson now versus waiting a quarter?" Mike volunteers.

"Or what if we decided to use a third-party online resource and LinkedIn instead of the recruiter?" Nancy asks.

I nod my head along with all the ideas.

"Sandy, would you be willing to try this latter approach until we dig into that analysis Mike mentioned?" I ask.

She agrees, and I turn to Mark.

"Would you be willing to take on the analysis and finish it by our next meeting?"

Mark gives a big sigh before eventually saying yes.

I look around the room.

"I'm not sure if that was the *best* process to get to an answer," I say. "But I do appreciate how we tried to solve the problem. Everyone shared their input, and we have produced some alternative solutions we didn't initially see. And that's great. Wonderful job, everyone."

"Remember," I continued. "Strategic planning is just a hypothesis, not a fact. This was a great example of that. But instead of punting the question and not getting anything done, we're evaluating new options and trying to find a way to get to a more positive outcome."

There are head nods all around. But I notice a subtle look pass between Mark and Sandy. Awkwardness lingers in the air a bit, and I can tell the two have a conflict with each other now. *Add that to my list of things to fix,* I think. I have to admit, I'm a little frustrated with how Mark uses his budgeting power to kill potentially innovative ideas — and generally zeroes in on those specific numbers instead of looking at the big picture or other longer-term analysis.

I push the worries about Mark to the back of my mind and take a look at the spreadsheet one more time as everyone leaves the room. Several green and yellows and only two reds left, now that we've flipped Sandy's back to yellow. Progress. Still, I can't help but feel like the boat is losing steam. It's time to call Charlie again.

Chapter 28

Tracking Your Buoys

Have time for a quick call today? I text Charlie.

In Boston with a client, he writes back. *But I can call you between our last meeting and dinner.*

A couple of hours later, my phone rings right on cue.

"Hey, what's going on?" Charlie says. Always jumping right into it.

I brain-dump for a few minutes — about the progress we've made, about starting two weeks later than anticipated because of the extra time spent clarifying the journeys, and all the status updates I've been receiving via the spreadsheet. And finally, I get to the reason I'm calling in the first place: the stalled progress.

"And I really don't know what to do next," I finished.

"Ah, yes," he says. "This is a really common problem. Have you laid out your buoys yet? The leading indicators along the way that tell you whether you're heading in the right direction or not?"

I think about this for a second. *He's right.* Even after everything Charlie's taught me — and as much as that whole buoy concept clicked when I first heard it — I realize I've been going about it *in practice* all wrong. I'm still measuring everyone's success based on whether we're on track to the end destination. All those red, yellow, and green blocks on the spreadsheet don't actually tell me whether anybody is taking the actions they're supposed to.

I feel like smacking myself on the forehead. *That's* what we should be measuring.

"No, we're not," I answer, explaining that everyone is just filling in status updates on the spreadsheet.

"That's okay," Charlie says. "That's more than many organizations do, so you're on the right track. But from here forward, your team needs to track progress against their leading indicators, *not* against a timeline estimate for the end result. Keeping track of those indicators should automatically let you know whether you're ahead of schedule, on track, or behind schedule. You won't even need color coding."

"What are some of those things we should be measuring instead?" I ask. "Take my sales manager, Sandy. She's behind schedule right now because we didn't factor a recruiter into the Q1 budget. So she's stuck on her journey of hiring the new salespeople."

"Okay, let's look at it this way," Charlie says. "Let's say to hire one salesperson, you need to interview ten people. You could use this as your oar. 'We're going to interview ten people by a certain date.' But an even better approach is to say, 'We're going to interview three people by week one, get that total to six people by week two, and finish the last of the ten interviews by week three. Monitoring those numbers will keep you on track with your efforts. Does that make sense?"

"It definitely makes sense," I agree. "But I worry that I'd be micromanaging."

"The journeys are all approved by the team, right?" he asks.

"Yes."

"Okay, so on a journey and oar level, the captain should be reviewing with their team members on a weekly basis their progress on each action step. The weekly meeting should be short, clear, and to the point. First step is to review the progress from the previous week. If they've met their intended progress, then you congratulate the captain. If there are obstacles or challenges, make sure you understand what's holding them up. If the captain didn't complete their actions from the previous week, try to understand why they fell short. Then move on to the next week's actions. Make sure the captain is clear on exactly what they need to do and what their team needs to do. Then ask if they need any help in removing obstacles."

"That all makes sense," I say. "Short and sweet."

"Exactly. Thank them for their time and move on to the next person. Then make sure next week's meeting to review progress is on the calendar."

"So what if someone is continually off track with where they need to be?" I ask.

"You need to make sure they feel understood, firstly. You can tell them you appreciate their challenges from the previous week. But be firm that you need them to get back on track the next week. Which means they need to finish last week's action *and* the upcoming week's action on a condensed timeline. Both need to be finished by the time you meet again."

"Wow, really?" I ask. "That seems a little harsh. I do get that sometimes there are legitimate reasons for not finishing something…"

"I know, I used to be wishy-washy about it myself," Charlie says. "And what happened? My projects fell behind. I allowed all those excuses to pile up and be the reason we never made any progress. I created a culture of excuses."

I thought about this. By being understanding, was I just setting the stage for mediocrity and slow progress?

"Let me share really quickly an experience I had after learning about this technique," Charlie says. "I was managing a sales team. They were effective, they took initiative. But one of their strategic journeys the year I was working with them was to create a sales playbook within 12 months. The sales playbook was a detailed procedure on how they should find leads, turn those leads into opportunities, and close the opportunity into a sale. I had other priorities, so I didn't actually get to meet with the team in person until five months into the year. Finally, we set up a meeting to go over their progress. I realized pretty early on in that meeting that they'd made virtually no progress.

The whole journey lacked any oars — let alone accountability. The team was meeting on a regular basis, but they weren't moving forward at all."

"So, what did you do?" I ask.

"I separated the salespeople into three groups," he says. "I told them we were instead going to create three different sales playbooks for three different industries. Each group would focus on their specific industry. From there, they'd develop their weekly action steps — how they'd row their oars, in other words. Each week from then on, I met with each team to go over their progress. Adding in that accountability step made a huge difference. Things started to move a lot faster. At first, they were surprised that I was going to show up every week and ask for their updates. But they didn't need to hear it twice. They understood I was serious about this being the expectation. They needed to pull their weight. So every week, we met, reviewed, celebrated the progress they'd made, held the people accountable who needed to be held accountable, and clarified next week's actions. And do you know what happened, Jack?"

"You finished all three playbooks by the end of the year?"

"Better than that," Charlie answers. "All three were done by August. They started to use them by September. Those new personalized playbooks specific to the industries they were targeting helped them be more confident in their sales process."

"Wow," I say, raising my eyebrows. Shaving an entire quarter off a strategic project was the kind of stuff I dreamed about.

"With 'traditional' accountability, we were just going to produce one sales playbook by the end of the year," Charlie says. "Looking back, I'm not sure if we were ever going to finish it, judging by the pace they were on. But when we changed our approach, we not only completed the original goal five months earlier than planned, but we tripled our output."

"I really don't think I manage that way, though," I say. "I've always really prided myself on setting a goal and letting my team figure it out. I want them to have autonomy. But at the same time, so many of our projects finish late, or they're not finished with the right quality I expect, because the team is just rushing to get them done by the deadline. Usually, I see a lot of exuberance initially at the beginning of a quarter and then... crickets. Then finally, at the end of the quarter, I see that frantic rush to complete a project. And of course, there's the rush of excuses as to why they couldn't get it done in time. Then I end up extending the deadline. From the outside looking in, I'm never really sure what else to do. Because since I haven't been involved with the project, I can't validate whether their whole process has been right or wrong, or whether a challenge they say they faced was actually that big of an obstacle."

"Exactly," Charlie says. "That was my experience before I started that cadence of weekly action. Actually, I still use this approach today with our internal team, and with our clients. It's not uncommon to see triple output like we saw with those playbooks — and with higher quality than we were getting before."

"But here's the amazing part," Charlie continues. "The team is happier. The people doing the work *appreciate* having weekly feedback. They're not just floating around in the dark wondering if they're headed in the right direction. Of course, they still get frustrated if they fail to hit that week's goal. But they now understand it's their responsibility to get things done. No excuses. Plus, when you work week to week, it's easier to solve the smaller problems. When you hit a tsunami of excuses at the end of a quarter, what can you really do about it at that point? Yes, sometimes teams will pull all-nighters and get the job done. But at what cost? Rarely is the quality any good when it's being rushed like that."

"Tell me about it," I say, thinking back to all the rush jobs I've seen thrown onto my desk at pretty much the last second of a quarter.

"I learned something else in this process that surprised me," Charlie says. "People want clarity. They want to do excellent work. They want to win. And a more consistent feedback loop means you can iterate faster, get more clarity on each of your goals, and build up a series of wins that gives everyone confidence."

"I agree with that," I say. "I don't think anyone ever *wants* to do a bad job."

"Exactly. And here's another tip: start with those wins that people are getting. I used to start meetings with people with the whole 'How are you doing? What's going on?' thing. For the first 15 minutes sometimes, I would listen to life issues and work complaints, thinking that I was being an empathetic manager. Then we'd be in a rush at the end to deal with all the actual pending work actions. But when we shifted our focus and started each meeting with the quick wins people had experienced, all those work complaints started filtering away. The complaints had always been based on their frustration that they weren't making a difference, and they couldn't get their jobs done. They weren't moving the dial. But when you remove excuses, and maintain accountability, people start to get more engaged. They see the results of their work — and they want to keep building that momentum. When people start winning, they want to keep winning."

"It's like those sports teams that start off a season undefeated," I say. "When they can build up that momentum and develop a winning culture in the locker room, everybody in that room wants to keep winning."

"Bingo," Charlie says. "And at least here on my team, now that our employees are happier, we usually spend time at the end of each of our meetings to dig into that human element. We hear about people's lives and what else is going on outside the office. Sometimes we'll talk about how everyone's families are doing, or if someone's kid scored a winning touchdown in their game. Because the human element is still huge. People go to work for a purpose, but they're primarily there to pay the bills. They're there to make enough money to pay their rent, or mortgage. They want to pay for a vacation or two, and buy a car they like. So at the end of the day, if they wanted to take on another job and go do something else to make that money, they could. But when you create an environment of success, and when people can see that they can provide for themselves and their family at your organization, but *also* do magnificent work, then that's an unstoppable combination."

I think back to all the meetings I've led in my time as CEO — way too many management meetings that have been a complete waste of time. I honestly used to think this was all just a part of the job. But I'm seeing now… those wasted meetings were just bad leadership. I wasn't being the captain of the ship. I was just keeping myself busy as the cook — listening to stories, being a counselor, providing some resources, but not actually solving any problems.

Maybe I am *the problem,* I think. I'm the anchor holding things back.

"Jack, are you still there?"

I realize I've been lost in my thoughts so long that Charlie thinks I hung up on him.

"Yes, I'm here," I answer. "I'm just thinking about how I wish I'd known about this approach earlier. I haven't been building in enough accountability into my management style. And I definitely haven't done a great job at developing that culture of success, or of celebrating the wins. I feel like I really need to change my behavior after hearing this story. So what else am I missing?"

"Well, let's get back to focusing on the buoys and how often you should be reviewing them. Because think about the purpose of a real buoy in the water: They're the difference between seeing where you're going, and just floating in the open sea with no idea of which direction to go. When the Navy special forces are training underwater, without a compass and signal guiding them toward the next destination, they end up going in circles and returning to the same place where they started. After you provide them the right equipment, they reach their destination with precision."

"Yeah, those are pretty important," I say, thinking of the last time I was on a boat. All that open sea stretching out ahead of me in every direction. With nothing in the water and no GPS on the boat… we would have been out of luck.

"Timing really is everything," Charlie says. "It's no different with strategic planning and execution. So let's think back to annual strategic planning processes. Many organizations do these regularly, but it's more of a ritual than anything constructive. It's like dressing up in a costume for Halloween. You're doing it because that's just what you're supposed to do. You're not actually doing it because it's a meaningful action that will have any significant impact on the rest of your year, or the years ahead."

"Tell that to my kids," I laugh.

"Hey, dressing up in a costume can be a lot of fun," Charlie says. "But it doesn't get anything done. With these strategic retreats, usually the team will produce a few key ideas, which may or may not actually be acted upon in the upcoming year. More than likely, they'll be forgotten about — just like that Batman costume someone wore to the party that was maybe a little too tight around the midsection."

"Well, hopefully they forget about that," I say with a chuckle.

"Exactly. Now think about the one-year operational plan and budget. Some organizations think of this as their strategic plan. Usually they just pay attention to whether or not they've hit their financial numbers. And they only check in on them once a year. Frankly, I don't understand organizations that take this approach. No one stays accountable to the goal when you're only checking in on it once a year — when it's time for yet another strategic retreat. At best, it ends up being a nice party."

I reflect on past years' strategic retreats and wince a little. Definitely more party than strategy. More ritual than meaningful, innovative progress.

"The next group of contenders are those who review their plan quarterly," Charlie says. "Organizations that take this approach tend to be more engaged. They care. However, there are 365 days in a normal year. That's about 220 working days. If something is going wrong, it may take 90 days or more to determine whether your strategic actions are actually moving you in the right direction — or if you're headed in a totally wrong direction altogether. For a small to medium-sized business with limited resources, this can create some really costly mistakes they might not even be able to recover from. So, three checks per year before the year is over is good. But it can be a lot better."

"What about board of director check-ins?" I ask.

"Yeah, for small to medium-sized companies like yourself, they might have a board of directors," Charlie says. "It's reasonable to share strategic updates with them quarterly. But internally, the best practice is monthly reviews. Sitting down each month to go over strategic initiatives with the leadership team helps everyone celebrate the victories, encourage one another to keep making progress, or potentially save the journeys that have rammed into an iceberg. Having more regular check-ins allows you to save the ship before it completely sinks. Throughout the year, you might decide to eliminate one or two. But even ten reviews over the course of a year is two and a half times more reviews than if you were doing it quarterly. That gives you two and a half times more opportunity for course correction."

"Wait a second," I say, confused. "I thought you were talking before about how important weekly reviews are? Where do those fit in?"

"Great question," Charlie answers. "The weekly reviews are intended to be more between the captains and their respective teams. Frankly, I think a weekly review by the full management team is probably too much. Oh, and we've also moved to ten-week sprint periods as our baseline. Usually those sprint periods fit within a calendar quarter — except we'll skip weeks that have holidays or a significant company event like a major trade show where key people are absent during the week. We usually factor in some rest periods between sprints too. If we're sprinting all the time, we run out of breath. So we build in that rest period and allow people to refresh a little before the start of a new quarter. The whole ten-week timeline usually helps us get a lot of excellent traction from quarter to quarter, plus appropriate rest at the beginning and end, while still allowing people to take vacation periods around holidays and feel less stressed. You'll get a lot done this way, but honestly, your team will really appreciate having a more realistic approach to strategic execution than just nose-to-the-grindstone every day."

"Yeah, this sounds downright easy," I laugh.

"Well, sure," Charlie chuckles. "It seems easy for me. It took nearly 30 years of work experience and hundreds of books and lots of blood, sweat, and tears to come up with best practices."

"Oh, is that all?" I ask.

"That's all!" he says, laughing again. "Jack, I have to get going, but keep me posted on your next steps."

As he hangs up, I start writing a list of what needs to happen next:

#1: Set up separate monthly strategy review with the leadership team

#2: Implement weekly reviews for each captain and their teams

It's time to get this stalled engine going again.

Chapter 29

Red Flag Warning

About a month and a half later, we're deep into our first ten-week sprint. All in all, there are far fewer excuses at the strategy review sessions. More greens and yellows on that Excel sheet, and only one red.

I'm starting to get the hang of these strategy meetings, too: two minutes for each leader to share their status update. Everyone answers the same four questions — what's your progress since the last meeting, what's your progress compared to the plan, what's your next step, and what are the obstacles or resource challenges you're dealing with.

Still, that one red flag keeps showing up with Sandy. The red flag is the signal where a journey or oar has stopped moving forward. The first time I asked about it, the response was positive: "Actually, we think we're going to be able to move in the right direction. Let's not worry about it yet."

So I didn't — until it showed up as red again in the next monthly meeting.

I ask the same questions, and get the same answer: "Don't worry about it, we've got it."

It's not the only frustration I'm noticing at these meetings. The spreadsheet we're using to track progress is starting to get a bit unwieldy, and a few people have even accidentally updated the wrong version. It's getting increasingly difficult to tell whether projects are behind or ahead of schedule.

Nothing is automated, and it was starting to get cumbersome to both update the spreadsheet — and *remind* people to do the same.

After the latest meeting, where I could sense the team's frustration about constantly having to manually update the file, I text Charlie. He'd already sent a text asking how things were going, and I responded with, "Good timing. Do you have five minutes?"

"You mean 25 minutes?" Charlie replies sarcastically.

He's getting used to this question by now — and to the pattern of jumping on the phone with me, then listening to me ramble way longer than either of us anticipated.

"No, really, just five," I text back. "Let's see if we can get this done in five."

Charlie calls, and I can hear the gate agents calling over the intercom. He's at the airport again, and tells me his flight is boarding soon.

As quickly as I can, I give him the rundown of what's been happening: the progress we're making in these monthly status meetings, the accountability that's happening among the leadership team, and the fact that I can feel us gaining more traction.

"But, we're still having a couple other problems. And I'm not quite sure what to do next," I say. "We have a sales journey that's in the red zone. And it's hard to tell what I should do, given that I'm only getting a two-minute update during these monthly strategy review sessions. The team thinks they can get it back on track. But this has happened twice in a row now. It keeps showing up as red, and I'm not sure whether it's time to start worrying."

"Could be a good time to add a 'Keep, Start, or Stop' review to those meetings," Charlie says.

"What do you mean?" I ask.

"Every six months or maybe even once a quarter, you'll do a larger-scale review of your strategic initiatives," he answers. "Keep the ones that are going well. That's the easy part. You're going to want to add in the new strategic initiatives that you've already started or need to begin. But even if you've already gotten a start on these, they need to get added into the strategic plan so that everyone can have visibility over resource allocation. Plus, you'll truly feel like the strategic plan reflects *everything* you're doing."

"What do you mean it has already started?" I ask.

"As much as I would like to say we control all projects and actions, a lot of decisions happen in the hallways," Charlie responds. "Next thing you know, a committee has been moving forward to tackle a project."

"I know exactly what you're talking about," I agree. "This process is a great idea. We already started tightening up our production process, which hadn't been in the original plan. But we should probably add that into the bigger picture plan, because it's turning into a really important piece."

Charlie adds, "When your organization is really dialed in, your team will think before starting that committee. The best practice is for them to 'ask' to start a new project to see if it fits in the strategic priorities. This includes you."

"Got it," I respond… knowing full well I'm the guilty party in adding new initiatives.

"Oh!" Charlie adds. "And when you're making these changes, make sure your strategic plan is in an easily modifiable document. If you start with everything in a PDF document, and then overspend to make it look pretty, you're way less likely to modify it. But remember, strategic planning is a hypothesis, not a fact. So your tools need to reflect this."

I think about our spreadsheet — not as static as a PDF file, but it's still getting pretty tedious.

"Now, the hardest part is to STOP doing something," Charlie says. "This is really difficult for executives, I've seen, because no one wants to admit that their grand plan isn't working. But sometimes, certain initiatives either need to be completely stopped, or they need to be pushed to a future period. The leader needs to admit when they didn't get it right. And that's okay. Again — hypothesis, not a fact. If we're trying to make big, meaningful changes to our organization, there's no way we'll get every strategy right every time. Sometimes we're simply wrong. Other times, it's just bad timing. Maybe we had the wrong resources, and need to push the initiative to a time when we can better align those resources."

"Strategic plans should reflect everything that's taking place within an organization," Charlie continues. "The good, the bad, and the ugly. It needs to be the lone source of truth. And sometimes that means cutting things. When we hang onto concepts that aren't working, it's just a constant reminder that we've failed, and that will just hinder your success in other avenues. For my clients, we do the Keep / Start / Stop process every six months — halfway between the retreat and the annual review. If you do this too frequently, you're at risk of making the plan *too* fluid and not maintaining enough patience for strategies that may take longer to show success."

"That's always been one of my weak spots," I admit. "Just having the patience to see something come to fruition. I always want things to happen immediately."

"You're definitely not alone with that mindset," Charlie says. "I've worked with some of the most successful people in their respective industries. I don't collaborate with slackers — only high-achievers. But still, even the best of the best fail. Remember, only 10 percent of organizations finish two-thirds of their strategic objectives. So you're in good company."

I remember Charlie mentioning this statistic over and over again in the time that I've known him.

"Why do you think that is?" I ask. "Why do only a tenth of companies actually do what they set out to do?"

"It's usually their past success that sinks them," Charlie says. "I'm not even referring to their strategic planning success. I'm talking about their individual belief system."

"What do you mean?"

"Well, why do so few people complete what they say they're going to do?" Charlie says. "It's because they're so used to succeeding, that when something doesn't work, they assign even more weight to that failure. Over time, as they fail to reach multiple goals, they accumulate the belief that they've failed. So then they don't want to take risks. But it's important to create an environment where we appreciate and learn from our failures. Because sometimes if we're going to try (and do) big things, we need to reward risk-taking. Even if those 'moonshots' — that's what I like to call them — don't work, at least you'll learn from the journey and apply those lessons to the next time you try something big or risky."

"I've heard of bigger companies building that kind of environment," I say. "But they usually have more resources at their disposal, right? Failure doesn't necessarily hurt as much in those kinds of companies."

"You're right," Charlie says. "Smaller organizations need to find a balance between those moonshots and the committed goals that they're confident they can move forward on, given their resources. But part of that balance means letting go of the goals that just aren't working. Otherwise, they're like anchors to your ship. They're mental obstacles — and the whole team needs to clear their minds of that quote-unquote 'failure.' It will impact their future risk-taking. There's no way we'll ever fully know whether something will work. But we can make adjustments when it doesn't. No need to overly scrutinize the people involved. They're probably already experiencing a lot of pain and suffering because of that perceived failure."

"That's definitely true," I say. "If we fail to reach one of our goals, I really notice the mood shift in the whole office. Everybody beats themselves up over it."

"Exactly, so there's no need to harp on any of that," Charlie says. "Now… if the team never applied themselves and showed no attempt to move forward or to change, that's a different story. You can take lessons from that situation too. Maybe you'll put different leaders on different projects next time, or institute more accountability, or maybe it will even show you that you need people on your team. But the point is to always learn from the initiatives that didn't work, and then apply those lessons to your future ones."

"Maybe that's what we need with this red-flag project," I say, halfway to myself and halfway to Charlie.

"It's possible," Charlie says. "You know, there's this belief in business that data drives our decisions. So a lot of CEOs internalize that belief and think that they should *only* make decisions based on data — and that there's always a clear-cut answer of what they should be doing. But honestly, one thing I've learned over the past 25 years is there's way more feeling than fact involved with a lot of decision-making. Humans are emotional beings. And strategic planning and execution are no different. So my personal experience has been: Let's get all the facts together, and then make a gut-based decision to move forward."

"Now, that's an interesting way of looking at things," I say.

"By trade, I was trained as an accountant and CPA early in my career," Charlie says. "I love numbers. But there are times when you have to recognize that the numbers don't always show you the right decision to make."

"Like when?" I ask. "How do you know?"

"Let me give you an example," Charlie says. "Many years ago, when I was at a manufacturing company, our executive team and board of directors made the decision to expand into a new, adjacent market. We believed we had to make only minor modifications, and our consumers would love the value of the product. The market data told us this was a massive opportunity. All the numbers were pointing us toward expansion into this market, so we did. But there was a big problem: our customer analysis was all wrong. They didn't want this new product at all. It took us two years for our egos to admit that we had been wrong."

"That's a lot of wasted resources," I say.

"It was," Charlie says. "That's why we need the Keep / Start / Stop process — so we can have flexibility to adjust our decisions. If we're thinking about the organization as a ship, we need the courage to leave the harbor and move into waters that we've never explored before. That's where all the biggest successes lie. But we also need the courage to throw out the life preserver before we drown, if the ship starts sinking. But organizations don't always see this. They become so emotionally connected to a failing decision. And this can bring down *any* business — from small company to enormous corporation. We *have* to stay nimble and on our feet. That's why we say…"

"I know, I know," I say. "Strategic planning is a hypothesis, not a fact."

"So get rid of any PDF document with your strategic plan on it if you have one," Charlie says. "That kind of document sends the message that all your decisions are permanent, which is the exact opposite approach you need to take. Instead, you want to develop a culture of learning that enables you to make the right changes when necessary. Sticking to a plan just because a document has been sent to all the employees and shareholders — and then being unwilling to change because of your ego — is simply unacceptable. But if we learn and adjust, that's what makes us successful."

"That makes sense," I say.

"You're a baseball fan, right?" Charlie asks.

Surprised, I say, "Yeah. I've been a Red Sox fan my whole life."

"When you go to a game, you want to see the home runs, right?" Charlie says. "That's why most fans show up. But they usually end up seeing a lot of singles and groundouts. Sometimes there will be a double, and sometimes there will be something as dramatic as a game-winning grand slam that makes the team's whole season. It's kind of the same in business. There could be steady things you're doing that move the organization forward that may not feel all that exciting. And then sometimes there are those grand slams that change everything. But you have to be willing to swing for them."

I roll my eyes, thinking of the last game, where the star player we'd just loaded up with a $30 million contract struck out looking. Surely I can take a few more swings than that guy, I laugh to myself.

"I have one more question for you before you jump on your flight," I say, as the noise of the airport increases in the background. "I think we can easily implement this Keep / Start / Stop process. But how should we be tracking our plan? Right now, it's just in a spreadsheet that everyone's manually updating — which is a step up from that PDF you mentioned. But it's still getting pretty cumbersome for a lot of people."

"I think it's fine for a lot of organizations to use basic spreadsheets," Charlie says. "But if you're focused on performing at the highest level, there's a better way."

"I think whatever it is, that's what we need," I say.

"If your team is documenting their weekly updates, this mountain of info can grow pretty quickly. So it's valuable to have everything stored somewhere where it can be easily viewed or modified. You want a tool where you can see both the big picture, and dive into the smaller details. You should be able to update weekly notes, track progress, attach documents, and hyperlink to other tools for more support. The tool should also be able to automatically sync from other systems, whether that's financial or operational or whatever other data you need related to your strategic plan."

"Sounds like exactly what we need," I say.

"You probably need an actual strategic software tool," Charlie says. "In my career, I started out with spreadsheets too, but eventually as I learned to track strategy the right way, the data efforts increased. With one organization, we were tracking strategy updates in Excel and Word, and we were creating presentations in PowerPoint. There would be replication errors. We were having to manually determine whether we were on track. We would have to share everything via email and hunt down file folders. It was so difficult to find the information we needed. Sometimes there would be a delay of up to a couple of weeks from the data input to the actual presentation. It started getting to the point where we dreaded making updates because our documents were so cumbersome. And our leading strategy indicators were already out of date by the time we'd meet again."

"Ouch," I say. "That's kind of where we are now."

"Well, at least for us, once we found a new strategy tool, our administrative time went down by about two-thirds," Charlie says. "It paid for itself very quickly by the time you factor in all the time — and headaches — we were saving. We only had to enter the info once, instead of three times."

"What a miracle," I laugh.

"Before jumping to a software tool, though, I always recommend that organizations commit to developing the processes and discipline around tracking their strategic plan," Charlie says. "Once that culture of tracking has been built, everyone will find a lot more value in software systems. You really don't experience that value until everyone is *highly engaged* in strategy planning and execution. You want to avoid buying into a software tool too quickly, when people aren't as committed to the strategic planning and execution process, because then you're more likely to get complaints that they can't do the strategy because they don't know how to use the software."

"We've definitely run into that issue in the past with other software tools," I say.

"Exactly. It's so common," Charlie says. "It's kind of like buying a Peloton bike. People buy those bikes hoping to lose weight and get in better shape. But if they fail to really envision the future healthy lifestyle they want to have, develop goals, design a sustainable plan to get there, and execute the plan on a consistent basis… what happens?"

"Well, they probably don't actually use the bike as much as they thought they would when they bought it," I say. I've been guilty of something like this in the past too.

"Yep. They don't get on the bike," Charlie says. "They don't have a process to actually use the bike, so they blame the bike for their lack of success. It's the same with strategic planning. If you don't build up the foundational pieces or build a culture of execution and accountability at your organization, your strategy is bound to fail. It's like when that Peloton bike becomes a very expensive towel rack. We want to avoid doing that with strategy software."

"I'd be nervous about that happening here," I say. "Still, I think we're starting to grow out of our current systems."

"Focus on doing the right things, then get the right tool to make your job easier," Charlie says. "That's the order of operations we teach. But a strategic planning software can bring huge value because it gets you updates faster. It empowers managers to make adjustments quicker if a journey is headed in the wrong direction. That can be really tough to do with some of the older, more manual tools that organizations use. But having the right tool or software with the right design can give your team a lot of clarity — and keep them accountable to your strategic process."

In the background, I hear the gate agent call for priority boarding, and I know it's time for Charlie to jump on his flight.

"Hey, thanks for all this advice," I say. "You've given me a lot to think about. It might be time for us to start looking at graduating past these spreadsheets."

Charlie laughs.

"Let me know what you decide."

Little did I know, that decision would have to wait — until I could solve the *next* conflict that was already brewing at the office.

Chapter 30

The Buck Stops Here

I feel like I'm pulling teeth.

That's the only thought running through my head, as I fire off yet another email to Mark to get the data we need for our next strategy review meeting.

I can sense Mark's increasing frustration. We're bumping up our tracking efforts, so we can stay on track with plan execution — but that means we're asking Mark for more analysis and info than he's typically compiled in the past. Before, we really only ever asked him for monthly financial statements, and to stay on top of accounts payable and accounts receivable. "Pay the bills on time, and let us know if we're headed for financial crisis" has been our modus operandi with Mark to this point.

But as our strategic planning efforts grow, so has Mark's responsibility. We need to keep tabs on all our strategic journeys and oars — and doing so means keeping an eye on all the resources available. It's a lot of forward-looking planning that Mark isn't used to doing. He's used to looking backward to last year in order to create a new budget. Even as the business has shifted over the years, we really haven't asked him to do a lot of forecasting.

Until now, that is.

And Mark is bucking up against the new expectations. He even expressed frustration with me last week that he wasn't a captain on any of the strategic journeys. He felt like he was just in a supporting role to everyone else's goals — and with more work than ever on his plate.

I'm in a bit of a conundrum. There's never a good time to make a change to your accounting team. Accounting is all about accuracy and trust. The one in charge should be a trusted partner of the organization. And they should be proactive: If things aren't going well, they need to be able to see where the potential pitfalls (or opportunities) are. Mark seems to be struggling with this forward-facing responsibility, especially as we've amped up our strategic planning.

This is exactly when we need future-forward planning the most from our accounting department. But Mark has voiced, to me, he thinks it's a waste of time.

"The forecasts are never right," he said during our one-on-one last week. "They feel like a waste of time and resources."

I tried to explain to him that strategy was *all* about needing to look forward. And how could we map out any of our initiatives if we couldn't plan our resource management ahead of time?

Should I find some part-time support for the more analytical information? I think to myself.

Most accountants, for better or for worse, have been trained in this look-in-the-rearview-mirror philosophy. Maybe bringing in someone solely for support around scenario planning and analysis is the way to go.

Charlie once told me that as a company grows, sometimes people who have been there for a while are threatened by that next level of growth. They'll fight changes, even if those changes are for the long-term health of the organization.

I'm starting to think Mark fits into this category.

And it turns out… he agrees.

Mark shows up at my office door a week later — and it's as if both of us know what's coming.

He sits down at the chair in front of my desk.

"Jack, thanks for taking a few minutes," he says. "I just wanted to be up front with you. You can probably tell there's been some friction lately between myself and the rest of the team. The further we get into the strategic plan, the more I'm seeing this probably isn't the best place for me. I try to fit in with all the changes going on, but I've recognized I'm becoming an obstacle. I had started noticing this a couple of months ago, but tried to stick it out and see if I could better align with what was going on. But a couple of weeks ago, I got a call from a recruiter, and long story short, I've been involved in a few interviews. I took an offer a few days ago, and I'll be leaving at the end of the month."

I nod slowly, the wheels turning in my brain. What could I do? It's not an ideal scenario to have to replace my controller right in the middle of a strategic plan — but at the same time, both of us recognize that he's been slowing our progress.

"Jack, I like you as a boss," he says. "I want to make sure to have a clear transition plan in place, so I'm not leaving you hanging. I'm here for any questions in the next couple of weeks to make things as smooth as possible."

"I really appreciate that, Mark," I say. "And I totally understand your decision. Alignment is important, and if you're not feeling that here anymore, then it's best to move on. Thank you for your honesty — and let's set up a meeting next week to talk through the transition."

Mark agrees, then gets up and leaves me with my thoughts.

As a company grows, I know attrition is a natural part of that process. And I can also clearly see how Mark has been an anchor holding us back from our full potential.

Still, the controller *and* operations director both leaving within a period of a few months?

What next?

Chapter 31

The Learning Process

Situation Analysis → Facts | Vision for Future → Where | CAPTAIN Program → How

A few months later, I know unequivocally that Mark leaving was the right move for Stackflow.

I brought in Leah as the new controller, and she's already making her mark. She'd previously worked as an analyst at a larger company, but had accounting experience at a smaller organization — the perfect mix for what we needed. On top of that, we brought in a general accountant on a part-time basis to handle some of the easier, day-to-day tasks, while Leah focuses on forecasting and analysis.

I took Charlie up on his advice to integrate a new strategic planning software, and Leah has taken the reins. She makes sure all the reports are updated consistently, plus she did the legwork to integrate the tool with all our current systems to make sure everything is in alignment. Tying in all our financial and operational data with the strategic initiatives has been a godsend.

And the results are showing.

We're not even to the end of the year, and we're already 60 percent of the way through our strategic objectives. I think about that stat Charlie always likes to throw out — only 10 percent of companies finish two-thirds of their initiatives — and I feel proud at how far we've come.

Sandy has really started to rise as a great sales leader, too. She's hired two new salespeople, with great results. Tonya has already won her first big deal, which means we already have a positive return on her hire. The second sales hire, Jacob, is promising too.

Better yet, we've already recouped the money we spent on the recruiter we hired.

It turns out that Sandy got the last laugh over Mark when it came to the recruiter. He hadn't wanted to hire one at all, but with a little research and financial forecasting, Sandy stuck to her guns. She knew the right support could attract the right staff faster, and we could get a quicker ROI. She found a great partner who had a different fee structure than the typical finder's fee approach — so we'd cut our recruitment costs nearly in half.

With all the extra support, Sandy's cleared the space to be able to get back to her sales roots. As the new hires work to add incremental sales, Sandy has been hard at work with our existing customers to add new sales. Today, our sales are 5 percent above our planned growth.

We've also revamped our customer service process, so those existing customers stay happy. It turns out, that's been a huge boon to our existing sales base. The top 20 percent of our customers have continued to buy more products than ever before. And since they were already larger customers, that impact has been huge.

Sandy brought up another great idea in one of our last strategy review sessions — what if we fractured our sales team?

"Hear me out!" she said. In the past couple months, she'd noticed that the sales team was… well, maybe a little *too* good at customer service. They would spend just as much time on a $3 sale as they would on a $300,000 sale. So, what if we split our sales team into multiple groups? One more experienced team that serviced those higher-level customers, and a second team that handled the middle tier? For the lower-tier customers, we automated quite a bit of our customer service processes — something I probably would have never considered just a few years ago. But that nimbleness that Charlie has been coaching me on is really paying off.

We did lose a few of these lower-tier customers, which ordinarily would have been scary. Any lost business used to turn into an anxiety spiral. What if that business was the difference between hitting our revenue goals and missing them?

But it helps to work smarter, not harder: Those higher tier customers that we were spending the most time and energy on routinely brought the most consistent (and profitable) sales. Our revenues were actually *increasing*, despite losing some of those low-volume customers. And our bottom line was holding strong — partially because of the higher sales numbers, but partially because we didn't end up having to expand our account management team at the rate we had been expecting.

"Maybe we should consider implementing a minimum quantity on all orders," Sandy mentions in our October meeting. "That might help us eliminate some more of these really low-volume customers who eat away at our resources, but don't actually add much to our bottom line."

It's a great idea — and maybe even a start to next year's strategic planning. Sandy beams with pride.

Meanwhile, Mike has stayed on in a more supervisory role, with less day-to-day responsibility. (Thankfully, it seems as if this has saved his marriage.)

Mike had also made a great hire in Paul, who's certified in lean operations and came from a company that had grown from $5 million to $35 million over a seven-year period. Talk about great wisdom to have under our organizational umbrella.

Paul's been excellent at eliminating waste — who knew we had so much bloat in our processes? It seems like we're finally starting to work smarter, not just harder, and that's truly been a win-win. Since he came onto the team, our manufacturing capabilities have increased 30 percent. And the best part of all: we're not going to have to start a second shift for another 12 months.

Mike's return to the fold is a great illustration of the way the culture has turned around at the office. We hadn't put employee retention into our strategic plan — but with all the changes going on, our turnover rate has actually been substantially lower. It turns out, employees want to stick around when they connect to a larger vision — and they're seeing consistent, measurable results quarter after quarter.

That's something I've prioritized over the last several months: sharing strategic and financial results with the whole team each quarter. I never want anyone to feel like they're outside the loop and wondering what on earth's going on.

The ten-week sprint periods (and weekly check-ins) have helped with that too. The whole team is more engaged with their managers, because — well, they kind of have to be under that weekly cadence. Every week, they have to show up with the results from their work, questions about what's upcoming, and details about any obstacles they're facing. Everyone's working with more clarity — and it's turning into greater outputs across the board.

All those employees have been talking, too. We've already built up a solid pipeline of potential future hires, based solely on internal referrals. That's something we've never had the entire time I've worked here.

This is the first time in my Stackflow stint that a *lot* of things have happened, come to think of it — including, most importantly, a successful strategic plan.

Not everything has happened the way we wanted. We had to hit the brakes on a couple of initiatives, like buying the new production tool and focusing on the next 20 percent of customers. But it's only because we've been focused on other things: creating efficiencies by eliminating waste, and gaining sales by focusing on the top 20 percent.

But this is the most confident I've ever felt at Stackflow — even though, not long ago, I felt like we had hit rock-bottom.

We're not totally out of the woods yet as far as profitability goes. But the momentum we've built up — and how much is still possible — is exactly why this *next* retreat is so important.

And I know just the guy to call for our pre-retreat prep work.

Chapter 32

Not Goliath

"I don't know what I was expecting," Sandy says. "But that guy is not it."

Charlie had just walked through the office doors, and was setting up in the conference room. He's here to give some insight before our next strategic planning retreat — after all these months, we've finally been able to get on his schedule for an on-site visit.

And judging by all the insight that they'd heard from Charlie this year (via my second hand telling), I think they expected a six-foot-five giant, with a loud, booming voice, and maybe a long white beard (filled with wisdom). That image would have squared with the ones they had in their heads.

To everyone's surprise, the guy who walked in was closer to five-foot-eight, with an average-looking build — and no facial hair of wisdom. But what he lacked in size and stature, Charlie certainly made up for in passion, strategy, and people skills. Heck, that's half the reason we had as much success as we've had this year.

"Well, thanks for the opportunity to come in and meet with you all," Charlie says to the leadership team gathered around the conference table. "I've been hearing about all your success from Jack, and I know he's incredibly proud of all your accomplishments over the last ten months. You've come a long way, and have a lot to be proud of. The year isn't over yet, though. There's still a lot of execution ahead."

"I want to start by hearing from you all," Charlie continues. "Looking back at the past three quarters, and everything you all have done and changed since the last planning retreat — what has surprised you the most?"

Sandy is the first to jump in — and no surprise there. As much as she's grown in her leadership this year, she's also become less hesitant to speak up, ask questions, and give feedback. The evolution has been awesome to watch.

"To be honest, at first I had no idea how this whole process was going to help me become a better leader," she says. "When Jack talked about his conversations with this new strategic consultant, I thought we were just going to get some watered-down tips and tricks. Frankly, I didn't think much of it because so much of the planning we had done in the past was such a waste of time. But we've really created a different culture around here."

Several around the table nod their heads.

"I think a lot of that has to do with the accountability we've built up," Sandy continues. "And it's about clarity. We really have a clear vision of where we're going, which I think we lacked before. And we have this positive feedback loop. We're excited to get together for our next planning session, because we've built up all this momentum and we really believe there's so much more we could accomplish in the future with what we've learned this year."

"I agree," Mike says. "Initially, when we first started talking about goals and numbers, I thought that could only mean one thing: more growth means more work for me. When we started this process, I was at a complete dead end. I was working nearly 80 hours a week. My wife was weeks away from filing for divorce. Maybe even days, let's be honest. I'd even applied for a new position that could get me back to a regular working schedule. But when we really narrowed in on the details of this plan, I could see this was all about working smarter, not just harder. It's an awful cliché, but in this case it really is true. We were so fixated on how things had been done before, that we thought the only way to expand our capacity was to add on another eight-hour shift. To me, this meant that my 80-hour weeks were going to turn into

120-hour weeks. But then we started thinking a little differently. We focused on what we could get *rid* of, rather than just adding for the sake of adding. That process really opened my eyes."

"How so?" Charlie asks.

"I was so busy in the day-to-day operations that I hadn't even been listening to my teams," Mike admits. "When I started asking for their input about this plan, and some of the processes we could use to get there, everything changed. Everyone gained so much more confidence when they finally felt like they were being heard for the first time. And all along, all we had to do was stop and ask. This whole process has done a lot for our manufacturing process, obviously, but it's also created this new sense of teamwork. We have several team members who have been here for five or six years — and maybe were on the brink of leaving. But now all of a sudden, they're working with this new energy and really feel like they're making a contribution."

"And as much as I hate to admit it," Mike continues, "I was the anchor who had been holding back our manufacturing growth for a long time. I recognized that I needed some help, and that's why having Paul has been so great. His experience has helped lead us to a place I never would have envisioned. I just had to have the humility to recognize I wasn't the right person to lead us into that future."

"That's an epiphany many leaders *never* get to," Charlie says. "Trust me. And it doesn't mean you're not a great leader in your own right — you're just better suited for a different position. When people can recognize that, it's truly a win-win for everyone."

Leah jumps in after a brief pause.

"I'm new here, so I don't have the perspective of how things operated in the past," she says. "But I've been a part of several companies, and seen the results — or better yet, the lack of results — from a lot of strategic plans. This is one of the first companies I've been at that's tried to connect the strategy to the budget, and then connect the strategic results to the long-term impact.

Those are threads that are missing at a lot of organizations I've been a part of."

"You're telling me," Charlie chuckles.

"This has always been a point of contention for me at other organizations," she says. "I see teams regularly doing one strategic plan after another, but they never pause to look at the real results. They just move on to start working on the next thing. But here, we're thinking about whether these strategies are working in the short-term *and* what kind of impact they're going to drive in the long-term. As you learned recently, Sandy."

Sandy nods, as Leah continues explaining: "Our new salesperson has had some real incremental sales for the company. But I know we want to keep tracking this to make sure there are real returns in a year or two or three, and we're still on the right track to our goals — sorry, destinations."

I smile. It took me a while to get used to Charlie's vocabulary and all his metaphors — but soon enough, the whole team picked up on it and started shifting their vocab, too.

"So, Charlie," I say. "What do we do next?"

That draws a big laugh from everyone in the room. We've accomplished a lot — and we don't want to just jump to the next thing. But we also see how much potential there is. And we don't want to miss out on it.

"Well, we're now at the seventh principle of our strategic planning process," Charlie says. "Let's go over the other six stages again on how to become a captain of your strategic planning process. Does somebody want to toss me a whiteboard marker?"

Mike hands one over, and Charlie stands up and walks over to the board we keep on the far wall.

"The first stage was the vision stage — where it's all about developing buy-in," he explains as he writes the word "Compass" on the board. "We do this by creating a long-term vision, which serves as a compass for the rest of your strategic process."

"Next" — he writes #2 on the board — "we 'Aspire' to do great work. We establish three-year destinations that serve as our stretch goals, plus one-year destinations that have a higher probability of success. This is our goal system."

#3 goes on the board.

"The third stage is the 'Plan' stage," he continues. "This is how we get from our current state to our future state. We develop journeys, which are our strategies. Then we identify our oars, or our tactical actions to support those journeys."

"Fourth is the 'Trim' stage. This is the method of focusing and prioritizing the items that will have the biggest impact, and have the highest level of success."

He writes #5.

"Next we 'Act,' and this is where we start truly moving. We set clear action steps for everyone on the team, and develop ten-week sprint timelines to drive forward momentum."

#6.

"The sixth stage is our 'Illuminate,' or our measuring system," Charlie continues. "This is where you focus on the leading indicators — or buoys, I like to call them — to make sure everyone stays on track for completing their journeys and reaching their destinations."

He writes #7 on the board.

"And finally," he says. "This is where you are now. The seventh stage, I simply call 'Navigate.' This is our continuous improvement system. This starts with celebrating our successes at the end of each destination, journey, and oar. Celebrate and recognize your team's efforts. Find ways to help people realize that the work they did is bringing your company to its desired destination. For some of those shorter destinations, simple thank-you notes go a long way. For the longer journeys, you might want to consider giving out rewards and/or bonuses."

"When it comes to the significant journeys, you should plan for big celebrations when you reach them," Charlie continues. "Take a moment with your entire team. Do something nice. Remind the team that it's not just all about work, but we're going to celebrate the successes too."

"That's a great idea," I say. "I'm curious if anybody has already been doing some of this along the way? Have you all done any kind of rewards for hitting milestones?"

"Usually if I see anyone making an extra effort beyond the normal scope, I'll take them out to lunch," Mike says.

"And I've actually already been writing thank-you notes," Sandy says. "I've tried to get better about publicly praising people, too. I want everyone to recognize each other for their work, and I realized that was hard to do if I was just thanking someone one-on-one."

"Awesome job, everyone," Charlie says. "You're already one step ahead of me. Make sure you keep that up. And always find new ways to celebrate — whether that's monetary, or some kind of experience. Just take time to enjoy the victories, and don't let that feeling get stale."

"So is celebration the only part of the 'Navigation' phase?" I ask. "Or is there more?"

"There's always a little more to it," Charlie says with a smile. "I also want you to celebrate the losses."

I can hear murmuring throughout the room as everyone processes this.

"What do you mean?" Leah finally asks.

"Well, big growth companies like Google do this to encourage innovation," Charlie explains. "The idea is that everyone should be shooting for stretch goals — which will inevitably fail more often than not. But we should still be celebrating that effort. Because that's the only way that true, breakthrough innovation happens. And along those same lines, there will be times that you make decisions that you think will work out, and they just don't. Along with celebrating the losses, you should also praise the courage to stop doing something that isn't working."

"Now," Charlie continues, "you can have bad leadership or bad ideas or weak effort. I don't believe all failures are good failures. But operate in good faith at the beginning. You should assume everyone is doing the right thing until it's obvious that they're not. If everyone is going through the right process and is tracking toward success, generally failure can be a lesson, not a stopping point."

"I like this," Sandy says. "I can already think of a couple of people on my team who are really going to thrive under this concept. They like taking big risks. Although, I can also think of a couple that might not take to this as well…"

"I'm glad you brought that up," Charlie says. "This is a bit oversimplified, but some of your smartest employees — those A-students in school — are not natural risk-takers. They may even try to avoid difficult projects that have significant risk. It may be wiser to put those more risk-averse employees on 'committed projects' that need to be delivered on time and within budget. Everyone else can stretch a little more."

"That sounds like me," Mike says. "I was always more of an A-student who was really responsible. Working on some of these plans that had a certain level of risk usually scared me. I always wanted to stay with what felt most realistic."

"And every organization needs those people too," Charlie says. "Meanwhile — again, this is oversimplified a little — the C-students in school are more likely to be risk-takers. They've learned that high risk can lead to high reward. Maybe throw a couple of those employees onto the bigger, what I call 'moonshot' goals."

"That's where I come in," Sandy smiles.

"And no matter who's on what goal, or what the goals are, it's important to have an After-Action Report for every journey to dig into what went wrong or what went right, and how everyone can be better moving forward," Charlie says. "You know, Michael Jordan said he failed over and over again — he missed the game-winning shot 26 times throughout his career. But that's not what the fans remember. They remember the six championships he won with the Chicago Bulls."

"Heck yeah, they do," says Mike. I'd forgotten he was a Bulls fan.

"But one thing Michael Jordan always did was learn from those perceived failures," Charlie says. "Another example is the Navy SEALs. Everyone knows them for their daring missions. But no one really ever talks about their meticulous planning, or that their thorough After-Action Reports are legendary."

"I didn't even know they did that," I say.

"The more we can measure authentic effort in our oars and journeys, and the more we can learn about how we could have done better, the more we can apply those lessons to future efforts," Charlie says.

Sandy raises her hand again, this time looking a little sheepish.

"You know, one of the worst tricks that I've seen salespeople do is that when they're approaching their sales goal for the year, they start pulling back," she says. "They do this because their quotas for the next year usually increase based on the success of the past year. So if they hold back sales to keep next year's target low, they'll start off the next year with early success — and there's no hit to their commission. How do we avoid that same issue with strategic planning?"

"That's a great point," Charlie says. "When I've worked with sales teams before, I explain it this way: You should always strive to be your absolute best, because you never truly know what's going to happen tomorrow. Sometimes that deal you're holding on to will fall through or get pushed out. Or maybe their competition will push a little harder, and you'll lose it altogether."

I cringe a little, thinking about how many sales we may have potentially lost out on, simply because our sales team had already hit their targets for the year, and were pulling back on the reins.

"So with strategic planning," Charlie continues, "we need a process. First, we want to make sure to celebrate our success and everything we accomplished. Second, you want to go through a learning process. How can you learn from your experiences over the past year to improve what you're doing? As you prepare for next year's plan, be clear that you're going to make some adjustments. The one-year destination should be consistent, and tied to the budget. However, you need to create a new three-year destination — you want to consistently push that carrot out. Here, let me chart it out."

He takes the whiteboard marker again and stands up to write:

Year One:

Long-Term Vision (10 years or greater)

3-Year Destination

1-Year Harbor

Year Two:

Long-Term Vision (consistent, with minor updates)

3-Year Destination (Year 4 from start)

1-Year Harbor (Year 2 from start)

"You want to continue to stay strategic, while always pushing your goals ahead, so there's no complacency," Charlie says. "It also keeps people engaged. Trust me, I've used this process with dozens of different organizations. And when they stay consistent with it, it helps keep them looking ahead — not just toward the one-year target. That longer-term focus will help your team think big, while the shorter-term targets keep them thinking small. And I don't mean small as in lazy; I just mean small as in achievable. They gain momentum by pushing toward their short-term goals, but they still have a carrot in front of them that keeps them pushing toward goals in the distance."

"Where does the long-term vision fit into all this?" I ask.

"Great question," Charlie says. "You should be reflecting on that vision every year. Now, this doesn't mean you have to stay in lockstep with every single detail of that vision. Things will change. Things will become clearer. It's important that you recognize when something needs to shift, or if you need to provide a little more clarity to a certain piece of the vision. There will be times — especially as you grow — when you learn things about yourself as an organization. Maybe you thought you were serving one type of client, but you should really be serving another. Or perhaps you should stop selling products to the entire country, and only focus on one region. Maybe you expand your product line to a new vertical market. Or you recognize you're more of a service company than a product company. There are so many changes that can happen. The important part is to recognize it. If it looks like a duck and walks like a duck, then it's a duck, and you need to adjust your vision accordingly."

That draws a laugh from the whole room. Time to add "duck-spotting" to our to-do list, it sounds like.

"At the same time," Charlie continues, "you shouldn't use that freedom to wildly change your long-term vision every year. Those changes should only occur with significant insights gleaned over time. There should be minor tweaks in the short run. But if you have too-frequent changes to the long-term vision, you leave the whole team confused. And it starts to impact the near-term journeys, too. Think about it this way: As we age, the vision we had for ourselves as a 25-year-old, versus 35-year-old, versus 45-year-old, versus 55-year-old can be remarkably different. As companies age, the same thing happens. It's okay for mindsets to evolve as we get closer to that future vision. But these should be gradual evolutions — not whole-scale 180-degree turns every year."

"What kinds of evolutions should we be on the lookout for?" I ask.

"Well, things like changes to your core customer, or core product, of course," Charlie says. "But it can also be about recognizing and leaning in to your strengths. If you see that your organization is really great at something, you should be applying those strengths more within your vision. Also, one more thing. As you get closer to your long-term vision, you may want to consider extending it. Unless you're planning on an exit — imminently — it's wise to keep some of your decisions on the long-term horizon. Stay flexible and consider what the market is telling you."

"What happens at that point, if we get to the end of the long-term timeframe, and we're nowhere close to our vision?" I ask.

With as much momentum as we've built recently, I don't think this is incredibly likely. But it's best to be prepared for every scenario.

"If you're unable to move closer toward that vision, despite every single strategy and resource and technique you have, perhaps that vision is just not your reality," Charlie says. "Or maybe it's the opposite: maybe there's a vision for you that's bigger than you even realize."

"There was a point in my career where I had the strongest belief and vision for my future. I was supposed to be a history teacher and a high school varsity football coach. But I was still working my corporate job. Matter of fact, I had built up a tax consulting business on the side and told my employer I was going to leave in five years after I'd built up my business big enough to supplement my teaching salary, so I could support my family. Keep in mind, at that point, I was a 30-year-old CFO in a fast-growing tech company. The CEO said, 'We'd love to invest in you — but not if you plan to leave in five years.'"

"Ouch," Mike says.

"Right," Charlie says. "This was one of the most difficult times of my life. I thought I had a calling to teach and coach. But after a few months, I agreed with my CEO to abandon my dream and keep learning and growing with the company. I had a tremendous amount of guilt. Initially, they gave me an opportunity to manage IT, and that worked well. Then I managed tech support. Then they asked if I'd be willing to help set up a distribution center in Europe. That went well, so they asked if I could manage our warehouse team. Then we set up our lean manufacturing team. Then they wanted me to support sourcing products in Asia. Wherever they needed me, I just continued to add value. I got promoted frequently, and my compensation grew accordingly. They were all incredible opportunities, and I'm so grateful I made the decision to stay."

"What I didn't tell you," he continues, "is I got to coach youth sports teams for 25 seasons and watch my four kids play. That's a luxury that would have been missed if I'd been a varsity coach and teacher. And meanwhile, the company was growing. During my time there, we grew 3.5x. And that's where I learned how to create and execute successful strategic plans. That led me to another company that grew from 70 employees to 450 in three years, and then to me opening the U.S. office for an international strategic planning software company. And that all led me here, with you all, today."

There's a beat of silence throughout the room, as everyone processes this journey. Nothing is ever really a straight line, and Charlie is certainly proving that with his story.

"At 30, I didn't have that vision for my life at all," he says. "However, all of that led me to my dream gig. And now I have a wonderful, long-term vision that's grown from all of that experience. I invite you all to approach strategic planning with that same flexibility and sense of curiosity for what's around the next corner. If we aren't willing to learn, we close doors and opportunities that could change our business — and our lives. I know this is my personal experience I'm sharing, but this kind of winding road is true for so many different entrepreneurs and organizations. Your vision changes based on success — and also the failures. But your vision should always answer the question: What does it look like in the future? And how are we going to make a difference in our workplace, our community, and the world?"

"That's a huge question," I say. "And I can see how that answer might change or shift a little from year to year, just based on what's happening in the world or the market. But are there certain aspects of the vision that you think should stay the same?"

"I'm glad you asked that," Charlie says. "Your vision should always be supported by your core values. Your core values should be authentic and resonate with your company's ethos. They should reflect who you are and who you're trying to be. Your employees, clients, suppliers, and everyone else should know exactly where you stand. Your values should be a differentiator in the marketplace. Actually, this is a great exercise for you to do, even if you already have your core values chosen. You should create supporting 'key behavior' statements for each one. Think of these as how that value is displayed through action."

"Can you give an example?" Sandy asks.

"Let's say one of your core values is integrity," Charlie says. "What is the Webster's dictionary definition of integrity? Does it mean you don't lie? Does it mean you're consistent with your words and actions? Make sure you're really clear about what each value actually looks like in daily practice. The problem with having unclear core values is it can cause a lot of frustration with your team. If a leader tells someone on the team they lack integrity, it might cause a conflict, because it's like calling your mother a bad name. But if we create key behaviors that define integrity, we can clarify intent. For example, we might say that a key behavior for integrity is that all our published documents are accurate and complete. Therefore, if someone wrote an inaccurate document, you can have a clear-cut discussion about that specific behavior — without name-calling or causing friction."

I see a couple of people in the room jotting down notes as Charlie is talking. It's awesome to see everyone already brainstorming ideas for their behavior statements — because they can already tell it's something I'm going to ask them to write as soon as we get out of this meeting.

"I have one more question as we head into this next strategy retreat in a couple of months," I say. "Do we need to create a new SWOT analysis each year?"

Charlie laughs a little at this one.

"By now, you should know my opinion on that," he says. "Absolutely not. However, if you still feel compelled to do some of the SWOT exercises because — well, you did it last year, and you need to do it again — then I would recommend just going through the same filter process we talked about before. Assign a weight to each item, based on probability and potential impact. Highlight the ones that are the most likely to occur or that will have the biggest impact on outcome. Those are the ones you want to focus on, just like you did this year."

"Got it," I say.

I, for one, will be happy to leave behind the days of hours-long debate and brainstorming about SWOT items — only to leave the retreat with zero strategy or plan attached to any of the ideas.

"And I assume we want to keep specifically tying the yearly budget to the strategic plan?" I ask.

"I'd highly recommend it," Charlie says. "That's the only way of making sure you have the resources to execute your most important strategic initiatives. When resources are a constraint, like with most small to medium-sized businesses, you can create scenario plans. It sounds like you have someone on the team now who's pretty good at those."

He nods to Leah, who beams. This *is* her zone of genius.

"For example," Charlie says. "A blue plan is maybe the base-level budget and strategy. If you exceed that base-level revenue, and you create more resources, move up to the green plan, which includes more or bigger strategic journeys."

Leah scribbles notes, and I know she's already excited about creating these in a couple of months once we nail down our strategic initiatives for the next year.

Next year. It's hard to believe we're already ten months into our first *truly* successful strategic plan — and that we're about to launch Year 2.

I look around the room, and take a breath. There's always more work to do. Always more problems to solve. Always more market chaos on the horizon.

But I'm proud to have this team around the table — and thankful to have a process under our belts that we *know* will drive success.

Epilogue

Reaching the Destination

Three years later

We've finally reached our destination.

Both of our key lagging metrics have been exceeded: $20.3 million in sales and $3.1 million in EBITDA. We hired an investment banker to evaluate potential options and received multiple offers that beat our EV goal. We ultimately selected the best match — not the highest price. I never would have envisioned us taking that route. But now I know we can reach our long-term vision with the *right* partners.

Our management team has started to mature — which has meant they're able to lead without me being present at all times. I finally have been able to get back to strategic work (what a CEO *should* be doing). No more slogging through the day-to-day activities like I used to.

And at home, this has meant longer vacations, more evening dinners with my family, and a significantly reduced stress level. The bigger number I can now see in my bank account has been a fun bonus.

But when I really stop to think about it, this bump in happiness happened even *before* we reached that $20 million mark. It took me a while to figure out why. But ultimately it's because we were *winning*. We adopted this new strategic planning method Charlie taught us — but it expanded to really become a strategic *operating* system. We consistently set our destinations, plan accordingly, and execute effectively. We win annually, quarterly, monthly, and weekly. We know the score, and we know how to win. We have taught these key principles at every level of our company. Winning has become contagious.

All of this means we no longer need Charlie himself to facilitate our strategic planning. He gave us the tools — and we run with them. But we still have a strong connection. I meet with his team quarterly just to stay sharp and make sure Stackflow is continually using the best practices to execute effectively.

In the biggest full-circle moment, Charlie has even invited me to speak during his courses and conferences as a testimony of success. It's never something I saw myself doing — but I'm taking that adaptability Charlie taught us for strategic planning into my own life, too.

Meanwhile, Stackflow is about to head into the next phase of growth. And the agility we've built up over these past few years is going to serve us in the next chapter too.

Charlie taught us a lot — but nothing more important than the concept of strategic planning as a hypothesis, not a fact.

That's the only philosophy that will *always* keep us moving forward. Because we have no desire to be left behind again.

Acknowledgments and Short History with the Author

Perhaps the hardest part of finding what to say for *Lost at CEO* is right now. There's no way I can properly thank everyone who has had a contribution to writing my first book. This in many ways is a key story of my life, being an entrepreneur, intrapreneur, working with entrepreneurs and executives in their pursuit to do great work and contribute to this world. So, this list will not be complete, and my humble apologies for those I have not directly mentioned.

As a person of faith, I would like to thank God. One of my favorite verses has been a testament to writing this book: "Consider it pure joy, my brothers and sisters, whenever you face trials of many kinds, because you know that the testing of your faith produces perseverance. Let perseverance finish its work so that you may be mature and complete, not lacking anything. If any of you lacks wisdom, you should ask God, who gives generously to all without finding fault, and it will be given to you." — James 1:2-5 NIV.

I started writing over two years prior to this being published. Shelved the first writing. Took a break to reconsider the content. Started over. This book has put me through many trials, and I still have much wisdom to be gained. I have appreciated the gift of generosity without finding fault.

My other rock has been my wife, Sarah. As high school sweethearts, we have had the privilege of raising four wonderful children, Ashley, Zachary, Tyler, and Abigail. Without her consistent pursuit to support our home and family, it would have been difficult to be present in the business environment. And she is not afraid to say the right thing, including business wisdom, even when it is uncomfortable. Thank you to Sarah and my kids for being there for me. This has been the greatest blessing in my life.

To my father who has passed, I wish you would have had the opportunity to read this. To my mom, thank you for having the courage to trek across the country from Lynn, Massachusetts — Lynn, Lynn, the City of Sin — with four kids and limited support to start a new life in Oregon. This created an opportunity for my sisters and brother, Lisa Hardwick, Jim Talty, and Sherri Strandy, to experience a new life that we would not have had without that decision.

Although my Merchant Marines Officer father was not present during most of my life, many others have played a fatherly role. In particular, I would like to thank the recently passed, Mr. Perry Reel, and their family, Jerry Lynn and sons, Perry and Justin, for being there for me. Mr. Reel was wonderful in that he did not judge my actions or comments as we discussed "how to solve the world's problems" while playing hearts at the kitchen table. He also provided me with a few nuggets of wisdom that I pass on regularly to high school and college students: Get a degree in people, know what you know, and get a great first job.

To my high school varsity football coach, Craig Ruecker, one of the all-time winning coaches in Oregon, his program gave me a desire to clean up my ways for the desire to play in the Friday Night Lights in a program with integrity. Thank you, coach. Roll Tide!

I have learned a lot from many different types of work throughout my life. Growing up, my family was often in poverty (as defined by being on free and reduced lunch at school), to have things, you had to earn it. At the age of 10, my neighbors, the Anderson's, took me on the Finnegan bus to pick strawberries during the summer; we earned about $.75 per flat. That created my first entrepreneurial opportunity: picking blackberries, which grow like weeds in western Oregon, and selling them to neighbors for $.50 per carton. When I was 14, I started working my first "real" job at the 185th McDonald's for $3.35 per hour. At the time, this was the busiest store in Oregon, Washington, Northern California, Idaho, and Montana. I learned by asking existing customers an important question, "Do you want fries with that?"

That did a number on my facial acne, as I made and served LOTS of fries. Thank you to one of our store managers, Guy, my brother-in-law, for trying me out to make a few bucks.

This was the same time that my mom started cooking in tugboats in Puget Sound and Alaska. For the next four years, I would be responsible for cooking, cleaning, paying bills, and yard work, when we did not have someone else at home for supervision. High school and college jobs included working at a movie theater, stocking shelves for soda distributors, installing energy-saving shower heads for the local power company, insurance sales for small business, front door reception at the University of Washington Athletic Facility, and UW golf range golf ball retrieval.

My best internship experience was with an entrepreneur, Steve Fast, from Fast Utility Refund Service. First, he shared with me Zig Ziglar audio cassettes, which helped me to learn. To be a leader you need to be a reader (or listener) and when you help enough other people get what they want, you will eventually get what you want. This also led us to franchising his business in Oregon with Mr. Reel, mentioned above, and we started the Oregon Utility Refund Service.

I had tours of duty at Coopers and Lybrand (aka PricewaterhouseCoopers), and worked with two small companies while being the senior-most financial person starting at the age of 24. I do want to thank my good friend Nathan McCardle, who invited me to join Corillian, formerly a publicly-traded internet banking software company, where we had five of the top ten banks in the U.S. By the age of 30, I was CFO for Lightspeed Technologies, where we grew the company 3.5x over a five-year period. It's here where I thank former CEO Jerry Ramey, who was one of the closest Level 5, servant-based leaders that I have met. He provided me the opportunity to expand into operations, establish international distribution centers, run the company with strong core values, and most importantly, learn how to properly do strategy and execution with the leadership team's Fortune 500 experience. Thank you also to Dan Meub for your extraordinary mentoring in leadership and strategy.

At DWFritz, former CEO Mike Fritz provided me opportunities to work in China, invest in other companies, and expand our strategy execution knowledge, but most importantly lead to our connection with Tom Wright, CEO at the Sydney, Australia-based Cascade Strategy. It's here where we not only found a great tool to manage our strategy, but also created an opportunity to open the U.S. office for Cascade. After establishing early success, including winning a deal with a Fortune 50 client, I took the opportunity to lead the office full-time. We had an awesome team establishing that U.S. office, and I would like to specifically thank Nick Cuddigan, Kyle Pfeiffer, and Rebekah Komar for their continued support afterward. Over this five-year period, I consumed nearly 300 strategy and leadership books. The research helped me to better serve our strategy clients, combined with my practical work experiences with over seven companies who have increased in size between 2x and 7x.

And that led me to starting my current company, 40 Strategy. I left Cascade Strategy to build 40 Strategy with the understanding that most organizations spend about 2 percent of their time on strategy. For one typical leader, that is about 40 hours per year: hence the name. Hire us to support those 40 hours and be 3x more effective than you would be doing it on your own. Cascade Strategy solved the software problem to track strategy; but the real challenge I am dedicated to solving is helping organizations design a plan that actually works.

In this journey to create 40 Strategy as effectively as we can, we walk the walk and invest hundreds of thousands in leadership, business, and strategy courses, talking with experts, and hiring coaches. Specifically, I would like to thank the individuals and their respective support staff: Jerry Vieira, Scott Ballard, Jessica Yarbrough, and Darren Hardy for their incredible expertise to help scale our company. To 3 Dawgs, Dawgs! Dawgs! Dawgs! To IBTS, thanks for your local support, as well.

In completing this book, I cannot say thank you enough to Cris Cawley from Game Changer Publishing and Ashley Scoby for their support, writing, editing, and publishing skills — thank you for your patience with me. At 40 Strategy, I would like to specifically thank Tonya Smith, Cydney Watts, and Erin Gibney for their insights, design, administration, and project management for this book. Talk about challenging journeys! Thank you to Momo's wonderful leadership and customer service with his team at the Starbucks near Top Golf in Hillsboro. Every morning, they welcome me like Norm from Cheers, where I spent many hours writing this book. But we finally all made it to the destination! Thank you. I (we) could not have done this without you!

At 40 Strategy, our mission is to positively impact at least a million people and 10,000 organizations to find a better way to do strategy. Most studies show at least a 90 percent failure rate for strategy and execution. However, there is the 10 percent who actually make it work. We help companies design their plans the right way, so they can be in that top 10 percent. And then, we offer the coaching and accountability to actually get it done. Our results have exceeded our clients' expectations.

To reach our mission, we support the Measure Success Podcast, where we talk with top leaders, CEOs, entrepreneurs, authors, and extraordinarily high achievers, about effective strategies that help define and inspire success. And thank you to all of our incredible guests on the podcast: you are awesome! I am so excited by the incredible community that we are building. A special thank you to a few of our most consistent raving fans, Linda Ramey, Jon Foster, Ben Heiney, and JT Mann. Thank you to guest President and CEO Mac Lavier, GearUp Sports, a provider of our amazing swag for our guests and another guest, CEO Lucia Robles, Lucia and Company, for personalized gifts.

To our clients, thank you for starting us stronger than we ever anticipated. We continue to exceed our near-term destinations and conquer our journeys, because of you. All of our clients are critical to our success.

However, we are exceptionally grateful for a few of you, who are some of our biggest cheerleaders when it comes to referrals and providing constructive feedback that helps us strive to be our best. A special thank you to Brad Triebsch, Managing Partner, CVP Capital Partners; Kenny Greene, CEO, Terrane; Don Lindsey, CEO, Precision Machine Manufacturing; Rita Forden, CEO, American Osteopathic Foundation; Seger Morris, DO, MBA, CPE, FACOI, FACP, Mississippi Osteopathic Medical Association; Daniel Patton, CEO, Rothbright; Dr. William Morgan, CEO, Parker University; Marty Mazzella, President, Ti-SALES; Aaron Fox, President, Oregon Manufacturing Extension Partnership (OMEP); George Linscott, CEO, Printed Energy; Michael Darwin CEO, Allagi; and Justin Buell, CRPC, Managing Director, Investments at Wells Fargo Advisors.

With our latest blog, Strategy 4 Saturday, a four-minute read on tactics and strategies to improve your business. We have designed the book as a platform to walk entrepreneurs and executives through their typical strategy experience and plant seeds to consider a more effective way. Our team has created a live, interactive Captain Strategy workshop to help businesses design their strategic plans in a group setting in a cost-effective way. And we still do our bread and butter, which is on-site strategic facilitation to design world-class strategic plans individually with our clients, including coaching and accountability to get it done. Sign up at 40strategy.com.

It makes sense. All we do is strategy.

We also have a goal of donating at least $1 million to charitable organizations by giving the first 10 percent of our net revenues. That includes 10% of the proceeds from this book. We are on our way to reaching and exceeding that goal. That's what gets me out of bed each day.

Thank you. I cannot thank you enough!

I look forward to connecting with you. To learn more about our CAPTAIN Strategy workshops, strategic facilitation, and keynote speaking, you can contact our team at admin@40strategy.com. If you have any comments about our book or if there is anything we can do to help you in your strategy journey to reach your destination faster, please reach out to me directly at carljcox@40strategy.com.

Lost at CEO and CAPTAIN Strategy Terminology

CAPTAIN Strategy Principles:

Compass (Alignment System) - Develop an inspiring vision to attract and retain top-tier employees, and build alignment to execute that vision.

Aspire (Goal System) - Create stretch goals, and establish "WHAT" you want to pursue — even if it initially feels out of reach. The goals should be in a 3 to 5-year timeframe, with a reasonable chance of successfully reaching them with extraordinary effort.

Plan (Strategy System) - Design a detailed, focused plan on "HOW" to scale your business and recruit the right "WHO" to help get it done. A strategic plan is simply a collection of all the "Hows."

Trim (Focus System) - Evaluate your objectives based on impact and likelihood of success, then prioritize the top two to three to focus on.

Act (Launch System) - Establish clear start and end dates and install 10-week implementation sprints.

Indicator (Measuring System) - Flip the script of how you measure success, and figure out the best key performance indicators to monitor that will ACTUALLY bring you results. Focus on leading indicators rather than lagging indicators.

Navigate (Learning System) - Use a "keep, start, stop" approach to evaluate initiatives, and design a process for iterating on your real-time experience.

Traditional definition:

Vision Statement - A clear statement that defines the long-term future of a company and/or organization. This should inspire the employees of an organization.

CAPTAIN Strategy definition:

Vision - This should provide a clear, long-term picture (10 or more years) of what the future will look like as a result of the work your organization does. This should include what the organization will look like internally as well as the external results of your efforts. Describe this in multiple paragraphs. This should not be limited to one vision statement. This is NOT a dream. You should have a slightly better than 50 percent chance of reaching your vision or parts of your vision.

Traditional definition:

Long-Term Goal - The outcome obtained from an individual person or organization's effort in a 3 to 5-year time period. According to various statistics, the success rate is typically less than 10 percent.

CAPTAIN Strategy definition:

Destination - The outcome that we are expected to arrive at within a 3 to 5-year time period. Through a rigorous process, our clients finish in the top 10 percent of likely outcomes. This is about mindset. When you board a ship, plane, or train, you expect to arrive at the destination.

Traditional definition:

Short-Term Goal - The outcome obtained from an individual person or organization's effort in a 1-year time period or less. According to various statistics, the success rate is between 10 and 35 percent.

CAPTAIN Strategy definition:

Harbor - The outcome or destination that we are expected to arrive at within a 1-year time period or less. Through a rigorous process, our clients experience a 90 percent success rate. You need to establish harbors to successfully reach your longer term destinations.

Traditional definition:

Strategy - The method(s) used in order to reach your goal.

CAPTAIN Strategy definition:

Journey - This is how you determine the best method to move from your original starting point to your final destination. There may be multiple journeys used to reach your destination. We call them journeys because it's rarely a straight line from the starting point to the final destination. We often have to adjust our journeys based on learning from the marketplace, our resources, and capabilities.

Traditional definition:

Tactics - The actions that are used to support your strategy.

CAPTAIN Strategy definition:

Oars - Actions that are used to support your journeys. We prefer the visual representation where your people, processes, and systems are actively working on specific steps to power your journey.

KPI - Key Performance Indicator

Key Performance Indicator - A quantifiable measure used to evaluate the success of a company and/or organization, employee, destination, journey, or oar in meeting performance objectives.

Lagging Indicator - This is the end result of your performance: for example, your sales, gross margin, and net income. After reviewing this data, you do not have control over the outcome because it has already passed. In traditional strategic planning, these indicators comprise 80 percent of the KPIs.

Leading Indicator - These are the controllable actions that lead to the lagging indicators. There should generally be a cause and effort, which should significantly impact the end results. For example, leading indicators for sales may include calling potential sales leads, performing a sales demo, and following up on sales quotes. In CAPTAIN strategic planning, we flip the script, and 80 percent of the KPIs should be leading indicators.

THANK YOU FOR READING MY BOOK!

DOWNLOAD YOUR FREE GIFTS

Just to say thanks for buying and reading my book, I would like to give you a few free bonus gifts, no strings attached!

Scan for Book Gifts

I appreciate your interest in my book, and value your feedback as it helps me improve future versions. I would appreciate it if you could leave your invaluable review on Amazon.com with your feedback. Thank you!